Readings in

TRAINABLE MENTALLY HANDICAPPED

Irving Newman, Chairperson, and
Stephen Feldman, Department of Special
Education, Southern Connecticut State
College, New Haven

Special Learning Corporation

42 Boston Post Rd. Guilford, Connecticut 06437

Special Learning Corporation

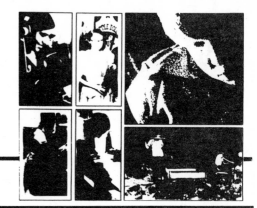

Publisher's Message:

The Special Education Series is the first comprehensive series designed for special education courses of study. It is also the first series to offer such a wide variety of high quality books. In addition, the series will be expanded and up-dated each year. No other publications in the area of special education can equal this. We stress high quality content, a superb advisory and consulting group, and special features that help in understanding the course of study. In addition we believe we must also publish in very small enrollment areas in order to establish the credibility and strength of our series. We realize the enrollments in courses of study such as Autism, Visually Handicapped Education, or Diagnosis and Placement are not large. Nevertheless, we believe there is a need for course books in these areas and books that are kept up-to-date on an annual basis! Special Learning Corporation's goal is to publish the highest quality materials for the college and university courses of study. With your comments and support we will continue to do so.

John P. Quirk

©1980 by Special Learning Corporation, Guilford, Connecticut 06437

First Edition

1 2 3 4 5

ISBN 0-89568-106-4

SPECIAL EDUCATION SERIES

* ● Abnormal Psychology: The Problems of
      Disordered Emotional and Behavioral
      Development
  ● Administration of Special Education
  ● Autism
* ● Behavior Modification
      Biological Bases of Learning Disabilities
      Brain Impairments
  ● Career and Vocational Education for the
      Handicapped
  ● Child Abuse
* ● Child Psychology
  ● Classroom Teacher and the Special Child
* ● Counseling Parents of Exceptional Children
      Creative Arts
  ● Curriculum Development for the Gifted
      Curriculum and Materials
* ● Deaf Education
      Developmental Disabilities
* ● Developmental Psychology: The Problems of
      Disordered Mental Development
* ● Diagnosis and Placement
  ● Down's Syndrome
  ● Dyslexia
* ● Early Childhood Education
  ● Educable Mentally Handicapped
* ● Emotional and Behavioral Disorders
      Exceptional Parents
  ● Foundations of Gifted Education
* ● Gifted Education
* ● Human Growth and Development of the
      Exceptional Individual

  ● Hyperactivity
* ● Individualized Education Programs
  ● Instructional Media and Special Education
  ● Language and Writing Disorders
  ● Law and the Exceptional Child: Due Process
* ● Learning Disabilities
  ● Learning Theory
* ● Mainstreaming
* ● Mental Retardation
  ● Motor Disorders
      Multiple Handicapped Education
      Occupational Therapy
  ● Perception and Memory Disorders
* ● Physically Handicapped Education
* ● Pre-School Education for the Handicapped
* ● Psychology of Exceptional Children
  ● Reading Disorders
      Reading Skill Development
      Research and Development
* ● Severely and Profoundly Handicapped
      Social Learning
* ● Special Education
  ● Special Olympics
* ● Speech and Hearing
      Testing and Diagnosis
  ● Three Models of Learning Disabilities
  ● Trainable Mentally Handicapped
  ● Visually Handicapped Education
  ● Vocational Training for the Mentally Retarded

  ●   Published Titles   *Major Course Areas

TOPIC MATRIX

Readings in Trainable Mentally Handicapped provides the college student in preparation for teaching exceptional children and the classroom teacher an insight into the special area of mental handicaps. It is designed to correlate with a course concentrating on this specific handicap, or supplement a general course on mental retardation.

COURSE OUTLINE:

Trainable Mentally Handicapped

I. Mental Handicaps

II. Trainable Mentally Handicapped
   A. The Individual
   B. The Family
   C. In Society

III. Trainable Mentally Handicapped in Schools

IV. Trainable Mentally Handicapped in Society
   A. Career Education
   B. Leisure Activities
   C. Self-Concept

Readings in Trainable Mentally Handicapped

I. The Trainable Mentally Handicapped: Rights, Responsibilities, and Family Concerns

II. Instruction and Training of the Trainable Mentally Handicapped

III. Assimilating the Trainable Mentally Handicapped Into Society

Related Special Learning Corporation Readers

I. Readings in Mental Retardation
II. Readings in Down's Syndrome
III. Readings in Educable Mentally Handicapped
IV. Readings in Vocational Training for the Mentally Retarded

V. Readings in Developmental Psychology: The Problems of Disordered Mental Development

CONTENTS

3. Assimilating the Trainable Mentally Handicapped

GLOSSARY

adaptive behavior The extent to which the individual meets the standards of personal independence and social responsibility expected of his or her peer group.

advocacy A program in which agencies or volunteers act on behalf of the interests of other persons who are in some way developmentally disabled. The interests of others may range from the services the individual needs, the exercise of his full human and legal rights, representation in society, to becoming a foster or adoptive parent.

amniocentesis Insertion of a needle through the abdominal wall into the uterus to extract amniotic fluid and diagnose the presence of syndromes or diseases which cause mental retardation.

amniotic fluid The fluid in the uterus that surrounds the fetus.

birth injury Temporary or permanent trauma sustained during the birth process.

career education The entire educational curriculum, coordinating all school, family and community components together to develop each individual's potential for economic, social and personal success.

chromosome Structures in the nucleus of a cell which carry the genes.

chromosome abnormality Any body in the nucleus of a cell that possesses genes which differ in some way from the normal cell.

cognition The process of thinking and intellectual functioning.

congenital Present at birth.

diagnostic services Include, but are not limited to the educational, medical, psychological, and social aspects of the individual that identify the presence of mental retardation as well as other related conditions. Diagnostic services examine the causes, complications and consequences of the problem.

educational objectives Measurable, specific student behaviors planned by the teacher in an educational program.

employability Possessing a "marketable skill", one that enables a person to be attractive as an employee in a work setting appropriate to his or her potential.

evaluation A process of arriving at decisions regarding learning abilities or behavioral levels of a student.

gene The parts of the chromosome which transmit hereditary characteristics.

genetic counselling Medical and therapeutic prevention of birth defects.

Individualized Education Plan (IEP) A formal written program developed by school personnel, a child's parents, and/or a parent advocate in order to delineate assessment, placement, goal setting, special services and evaluation procedures.

mainstreaming The placement of handicapped students into educational programs with normally functioning students.

mental age Level of measured or judged mental ability as shown on an intelligence test.

moderate mental retardation see "trainable mental retardation."

normalization The opportunity of an individual to function in as normal a setting as possible, to realize his or her potential and to maintain behaviors and characteristics which are as culturally normal as possible.

post natal After birth.

pre natal Before birth.

psychomotor Pertaining to the physical or motor effect of psychological processes.

rubella A disease which, if contracted by the mother during the first three months of pregnancy can cause congenital defects in her offspring. Commonly known as German Measles.

sheltered workshop A facility which provides occupational training and/or protective employment.

social learning Increasing a child's competence in making relevant decisions and exhibiting appropriate behavior.

special class A self contained classroom providing special instruction to mentally handicapped students and others with special needs.

syndrome A collection of specific symptoms.

trainable mentally retarded A condition that causes one, at maturity, to be unable to attain an intellectual functioning greater than that commonly expected of a seven year old child, but greater than that of a four year old child.

PREFACE

It has been estimated by many that approximately 3% of the American population is mentally handicapped. According to the American Association on Mental Deficiency (AAMD), mentally handicapped refers to subaverage intellectual functioning described in the past as an IQ score at least two standard deviations below the mean IQ of 100; (since each standard deviation is 15 points, this would mean an IQ score of below 70) and deficits in adaptive behavior (getting along in society, adapting to new situations, interacting with others.)

The overall majority (approximately three-quarters) of these mentally retarded individuals fall into the "educable" or mildly handicapped range. A smaller number (less than one-quarter) fall into the trainable or moderately handicapped range.

This book deals with the trainable population. In general, the trainable mentally handicapped should be challenged to reach their full potential, should be trained vocationally and should be accepted as people with needs, concerns and worth.

Basically, the trainable mentally handicapped will need support from others all of their lives, require a somewhat sheltered existence and will need guidance in order to survive.

Trainable mentally handicapped individuals are dependent on caring families, effective schools and efficient programs. Most of all, they need understanding and public awareness. They are entitled to live useful and pleasurable lives--free of prejudice, ignorance and neglect.

The Trainable Mentally Handicapped: Rights, Responsibilities and Family Concerns

Under Public Law 94-142, (The Education of All Handicapped Children Act of 1976) every individual receiving special education in America is entitled to a free, appropriate education. For the trainable mentally handicapped individual, this means meaningful programs and training. Vocational potential must be tapped and utilized; and for many, functional education and useful careers are possible for the first time. Parents of the handicapped are becoming aware of these rights and have been aware of the responsibilities involved in raising trainable mentally handicapped children.

The concerns of parents of the trainable mentally handicapped now include all of the above along with future prevention of mental handicaps through genetic counseling and overall awareness.

Most importantly, trainable mentally handicapped students must be challenged to reach full potential without expectations of the impossible. Aspirations far beyond the abilities of the trainable mentally retarded can do as much damage as expecting too little.

In today's schools, trainable mentally handicapped students can be prepared for realistic and meaningful vocational production and appropriate social awareness.

WHAT IS MENTAL RETARDATION?

From *Mental Retardation: Past and Present*, The President's Committee on Mental Retardation, U.S. Department of Health, Education and Welfare, Washington, D.C. 1977.

Mental retardation presents itself in so many forms, degrees, and conditions, from so many known and unknown causes, with so many questions unanswered, that it is difficult to say clearly: these are the people who are retarded and this is what they can do, and this what we can do for them, and this is how we can eliminate the problem.

To reach into the problem we have to know what it is.

To reach the people who have the problem we have to know who they are, how to understand them and how to help them.

Who Are They?

Mental retardation refers to significantly subaverage general intellectual functioning existing concurrently with deficits in adaptive behavior, and manifested during the developmental period.

This is the formal definition published by the American Association on Mental Deficiency in 1973 and widely accepted today. It identifies mental retardation with subnormality in two behavioral dimensions—intelligence and social adaptation—occurring before age 18. The definition is a culmination of long debate and revision, and may well be modified in the future.

The severely retarded person has an obvious incapacity to exercise the expected controls of reason and of personal management necessary for normal living in any human culture. Left to himself, anyone so impaired cannot easily survive. The great majority of severely retarded individuals also have physical characteristics which suggest a central nervous system defect as the basis of the developmentally retarded behavior.

In many cases no detectable physical pathology accompanies the deficiency of intelligence and adaptation. The limited ability to learn, to reason and to use "common sense" is often unexplainable. Can undetected physical pathology be assumed?

Further questions arise when we discover that milder degrees of intellectual and adaptive deficit are commonly associated with particular families who have serious social and economic problems. Do poor living conditions produce mental retardation, or is it the reverse? Or does each condition compound the other? Still fur-

ther, members of certain minority groups tend to be highly represented among those identified as having intellectual and adaptive problems, especially in the school-age years. Is such overrepresentation of certain groups a product of racial inferiority or of racial and ethnic discrimination and disadvantage?

For a long time, mental retardation (or its earlier terms idiocy, feeblemindedness and the like), was thought to have much in common with insanity, epilepsy, pauperism and social depravity, all of which were lumped together. And so, a concept of mental deficiency in terms of social deviance developed.

Then, as knowledge advanced, retardation was identified with congenital brain defect or damage, and assigned to heredity. This approach led to redefining mental deficiency in medical terms as an organic defect producing inadequate behavior. Mild forms of intellectual "weakness" became associated with forms of immoral behavior and social disturbance (the "moral imbecile"), and ascribed to more subtle defects of inherited character. Legal definitions in terms of social behavior began to appear.

During the 19th and early 20th century what we now call "mild" retardation was not recognized except as associated with disturbed or delinquent behavior. There was no simple way of diagnosing the more mild or incipient forms of mental retardation until the development of psychometrics around 1910. Then the "IQ" rapidly became a universal means, not only of identifying mental deficiency, but also of measuring its severity.

Goddard, in 1910, in applying the new techniques of Binet and Simon in the public schools, discovered there were ten times as many feebleminded as anyone had suspected, and promptly coined the term "moron" to cover them! Thus a psychometric definition of retardation came into being.

The intelligence test actually measured behavioral performance on tasks assumed to be characteristic of the growth of children's ability at successive ages, but it was interpreted as a measure of capacity for intellectual growth and therefore as a predictor of future mental status. It was assumed to represent an inherent and usually inherited condition of the brain with a fixed developmental potential.

Persistent debate over the nature and composition of intelligence finally led to an operational definition that it is "whatever an intelligence test measures." Since intelligence measurements are scalar, and degrees on the scale were found to correlate rather well with other clinical and social evidences of mental proficiency, low IQ became virtually the sole basis for a diagnosis of mental retardation and for its classification at levels of severity from "borderline" to "idiot."

This measurement was especially important in schools for which, in fact, the first tests were devised by Binet and Simon. IQ tests became the standard means of determining school eligibility and classification. Intelligence tests also were used extensively as sole evidence for determining legal competency and institutional commitment, as well as the subclassifications of institutional populations. The leading authorities, Tredgold, Goddard, Porteus, Penrose, Doll, Clarke and Clarke, all rejected a strictly psychometric definition, but it nevertheless became standard practice in diagnosis and classification.

In the meantime, research in twins, siblings and unrelated children had shown that general intelligence (i.e., measured IQ) is strongly inherited as a polygenic characteristic, following a normal Gaussian curve of frequency distribution in the general population. A slight negative skew was attributable to brain damage or genetic mutation. This deviation led to a theory of mental retardation which divided it into two major groups on the basis of presumed causation. One group consisted of the more severely deficient type with brain damage or gross genetic anomaly characterized by various physical abnormalities and IQ generally of 55 or less. The other group consisted of the lower portion of the negative tail on the normal curve of distribution of polygenic intelligence with IQ between 50 or 55 and 70 or 80 and not otherwise abnormal (Kanner, 1957, Zigler, 1967). This theory could explain the association of milder forms of low intelligence with low socio-economic status and its concomitants. In other words, the less competent tend to sink to the bottom of the social scale in a competitive society. The issue of cultural bias was raised immediately, however, with respect to racial and ethnic groups who scored consistently lower on the standard tests.

Evidence began to accumulate which generated a variety of additional controversial issues. The "constancy of the IQ" was questioned on both statistical and experimental grounds. The pioneering work of Skeels, Skodak, Wellman, and others, in the 1930's (e.g., Skeels, et al., 1938) had indicated that measured intelligence as well as other observable behavior could be substantially modified by drastic changes in the social environment of young children. The quality of the infant's nurture was found to have enduring effects of intellectual functioning, especially in the absence of detectable brain pathology.

Follow-up studies of persons released from institutional care and of those who had been identified in school as retarded showed high rates of social adaptation, upward mobility and even substantial increases in measured intelligence in adult years (Cobb, 1972). Epidemiological studies have consistently shown a "disappearance" of mildly retarded persons in the adult years.

Explanations for these findings could be offered without abandoning previous assumptions: Improvement in low IQ scores over several repetitions simply exemplifies the statistical regression toward the mean, inherent in errors of measurement: those who improve with stimulation and environmental change were never "really" retarded, but exhibit "pseudo-retardation" which masks true capacity.

Eventually, evidence converged to show that measured intelligence is modifiable within limits, that it is not in any case a measure of fixed capacity, but of the continuity of a developing intellectual and social competence in which "nature" and "nurture" are inseparable components and individual "growth curves" may take a variety of forms and may be influenced by many factors.

A gradual trend developed toward the

definition of mental retardation in functional rather than in structural terms and not tied either to specific cause or to unchangeable status. There were those, however, who continued to find a dual view of retardation more credible than a single continuum.

The Stanford-Binet and similar measures of intelligence came to be recognized as primarily predictive of school performance of an academic or abstract nature requiring language skills, and less predictive of other non-verbal types of behavior. Consequently, the need developed to measure other dimensions of behavior. The Army "Beta" test of World War I anticipated this development. New tests, such as the Wechsler series, combined linguistic with non-linguistic performance or quantitative elements and yielded a "profile" of distinguishable mental traits. Factor analysis of measures of intellectual behavior had demonstrated that "intelligence" is not a single trait but a composite of many distinguishable functions.

The measurement of adaptive behavior presented even greater difficulty. Such measures as the Vineland Social Maturity Scale were extensively used but had only a limited validity. The Gesell Infant Development Scale, the Gunzburg Progress Assessment Chart, and subsequently, the AAMD Adaptive Behavior Scale all attempted to measure the non-intellectual dimensions of developmental adaptation but they lacked the precision and reliability of the intelligence measures. Consequently, there has been a continuing reliance, especially in the schools, on measures of IQ alone as the criterion for mental retardation. This practice is defended by some authorities as legitimate in the absence of better measures of adaptive behavior (Conley, 1973.)

In the meantime the issue of cultural bias became an increasingly serious problem. All measures of either intelligence or of adaptive behavior reflect social learning, hence tend to be culture-bound. Their validity, therefore, is dependent on the cultural population on which the norms have been standardized. No one has succeeded in developing a universally applicable "culture-free" test of behavior. Attempts to devise "culture-fair" tests which employ comparable but culturally different elements have as yet failed to yield valid bases of comparison.

Recent studies by Mercer (1973 and 1974) and others have shown the extent to which cultural bias affects the frequency with which members of minority cultures are labeled "retarded" and assigned to special education classes. This is especially true when only measures of IQ are used; representatives of lower socio-economic and of Black, Mexican-American, Puerto Rican, Indian and other ethnic groups are identified as retarded far out of proportion to their numbers in comparison with middle-class Anglo children. Social evaluations of such children show that a high proportion are not significantly impaired in their adaptation in non-school environments.

This discovery has led to a coining of the term "Six-Hour Retarded Child," meaning a child who is "retarded" during the hours in school, but otherwise functions adequately (PCMR: *The Six-Hour Retarded Child*, 1970).

Mercer has called such persons who are identified in one or two contexts but not in others the "situationally retarded," in contrast to the "comprehensively retarded," who are identified as such in all the contexts in which they are evaluated. "Situational retardation" occurs by far most frequently in school settings, and next most frequently in medical settings, and much less frequently in ratings by families or neighbors or in settings officially responsible for the comprehensively retarded. "We conclude," Mercer says, "... that the situational retardate is primarily the product of the labeling process in formal organizations in the community, especially the Public Schools" (Mercer, 1973).

The work of Mercer and others has led to litigation and legislative action, especially in California, limiting the use of IQ tests as the sole criterion for labeling and special class placement, on the ground that such practices systematically penalize minority groups and violate their rights to equal educational opportunity (Mercer, 1974).

The present tendency is to accept the 1973 AAMD formulation by Grossman which requires *both* an IQ of less than 70 *and* substantial failure on a measure of adaptive behavior. The requirement of age of onset prior to 18 is more open to question and not always regarded as critical. The Grossman formulation differed from the AAMD definition of Heber (1961) principally in requiring a criterion of more than two standard deviations below the mean, rather than more than one s.d., as Heber had proposed. This was an extremely important difference because it excluded the "borderline" category which accounted for about 13% of the school age population!

Mental retardation, by any of the proposed criteria, occurs with varying degrees of severity. Many attempts were made in the past to classify differences of severity, usually on the basis of social adaptation or academic learning criteria. Social adaptation criteria distinguished borderline feebleminded, moron, imbecile and idiot. Academic Criteria distinguished slow learner, educable, trainable (with no term suggesting learning capability for the still lower category). Heber (1958) proposed using neutral terms to indicate standard deviation units on the continuum of the IQ and any other scales employed. This is continued in the Grossman (1973) AAMD system to categorize levels of intellectual functioning, thus:

Level of Function	Upper S.D. Limit	Stanford Binet IQ/ (S.D. = 16)	Wechsler IQ (S.D. = 15)
Mild	−2.0	67–52	69–55
Moderate	−3.0	51–36	54–40
Severe	−4.0	35–20	39–25 (extrap.)
Profound	−5.0	19 and below	24 and below (extrap.)

Note that the borderline category (−1.0 to −2.0 s.d.) is not included under the definition.

Mercer has identified still another variable of a significant sociological nature. A majority of children who rated low on both IQ and adaptive measures by the Grossman criteria, and therefore technically "retarded," came from homes that did not conform to the prevailing cultural pattern of the community (socio-culturally nonmodal). This group appeared to be identified as retarded more because of cultural difference than because of inadequate developmental adaptation. Further evidence showed that members of this group who were identified as retarded children tended more than the socio-cultural modal group to "disappear" as identifiably retarded on leaving school.

Mental retardation, as an inclusive concept, is currently defined in *behavioral* terms involving these essential components: *intellectual functioning, adaptive behavior* and *age of onset.* The causes of retardation are irrelevant to the definition, whether they be organic, genetic, or environmental. What is indicated is that at a given time a person is unable to conform to the intellectual and adaptive expectations which society sets for an individual in relation to his peers. In this sense, mental retardation is a reflection of social perception aided by a variety of clinical and nonclinical techniques of identification.

Within this broad functional definition, the deficits indicated in a diagnosis of mental retardation may or may not be permanent and irreversible. They may or may not be responsive to intervention. They may persist only so long as the person remains in a culturally ambiguous situation, or at the other extreme, they may be of life-long duration. Or perhaps only their consequences may be ameliorated in greater or lesser degree, not the condition itself.

Consequently, it is difficult to estimate how frequently mental retardation occurs and how many retarded people there are.

How Big Is the Problem?

The *incidence* of a disorder refers to the frequency of occurrence within a given period of time. For example, the incidence of smallpox in the United States might be expressed as the number of cases in a specific year per 100,000 population; the incidence of Down's syndrome might be expressed as the average number of cases per year per 1,000 live births. The purpose of determining incidence is to yield information as to the magnitude of the problem with a view to its prevention and to measure the success of preventive programs.

The *prevalence* of a disorder refers to the number of cases existing at a specified time in a specified population and is usually expressed as a percentage of that population or as a whole number. Thus, the prevalence of *diabetes mellitus* in the United States might be expressed either as the percent or as a whole number of the total population known or estimated to have the disease in a designated year. The prevalence of people crippled from poliomyelitis can be expressed as a gradually decreasing figure as the result of the greatly reduced incidence of the disease following the discovery of the vaccines. This shows that prevalence is derived from incidence, but modified by the extent to which cases disappear by death, recovery or inaccessibility. The value of prevalence rates is in determining the magnitude of the need for care, treatment, protection or other services.

Incidence

By definition mental retardation can be diagnosed only after birth when appropriate behavioral indices have developed sufficiently for measurement. During gestation the identification of certain conditions usually or invariably associated with mental retardation may be detected and *potential* retardation inferred.

From the examination of spontaneously aborted fetuses, it is estimated that probably 30 to 50 percent are developmentally abnormal and that if they had survived many would have been mentally deficient; but this information gives us only an incidence of fetal mortality and morbidity, with an estimate of some types of developmental deviation, not an incidence of mental retardation itself.

The mortality rates of the potentially or actually retarded vary with severity of defect, which means that many developmentally impaired infants die before retardation has been, or even can be, determined. Anencephaly, for example, is complete failure of brain cortex to develop; the infant may be born living and exhibit a few responses typical of the neonate, but survival is brief. Is such a case to be counted as an instance of incipient mental retardation or only of anencephaly in particular or birth defect in general?

Since mental retardation manifests itself at different ages and under different conditions, there is no single time—e.g., at birth or at one year of age—when it can be determined of every child that he is or *ever will be* identified as mentally retarded.

Mildly mentally retarded persons are most frequently identified, if at all, during school years, and frequently disappear as recognizably retarded after leaving school.

The methods of identifying retardation are still highly varied; consequently, surveys of incidence or prevalence are frequently not comparable.

The degree of subnormality employed as criterion for identification as retarded greatly affects the count of incidence. For example, the 1961 AAMD definition used a criterion of standard deviation greater than one (S.B. IQ $<$ 85). The 1973 version uses a more restricted criterion of more than two standard deviations (S.B. IQ $<$ 68). This change in criterion reduces the incidence of mild mental retardation automatically by 80%!

A similar problem is created by the use of multiple dimensions rather than a single dimension. If only IQ is employed, say at two standard deviations (IQ $<$ 68 or 70), a global incidence of about 3% of school-age population will be found (cf. Conley 1973). But if a second dimension of impaired adaptive behavior is also required, then some with IQ below 70 will not be classified mentally retarded, and some with low adaptive scores, but IQ above 70, will not be classified as retarded. This reduces the obtained prevalence rate to more nearly 1%. If, following Mercer, a still further determination is made on the basis of "socio-cultural modality" the rate may be still further reduced in some heterogeneous communities.

Taking many such considerations into account, Tarjan and others (1973) estimate that approximately 3 percent of annual births may be expected to "acquire" mental retardation at some time in their lives, of which 1.5% would be profoundly, 3.5% severely, 6.0% moderately and 89% mildly retarded. Currently, however, in view of the problems of arriving at truly meaningful estimates of the incidence of mental retardation on a global basis, emphasis for purposes of prevention is placed on the incidence from specific known causes. Unfortunately, these comprise only a small proportion of the total identified as retarded (Penrose, 1963; Holmes et al, 1965). The following are examples.

One of the earliest success stories in the reduction of the incidence of mental retardation was in the case of endemic cretinism. This condition occurred rather frequently in certain localities, notably some of the Swiss alpine valleys. The problem was attacked in the second half of the 19th century. The first step was to identify the condition with the occurrence of goiter, an enlargement of the thyroid gland. The next step was to relate this condition to the people's diet, and finally to the absence of trace iodine in the soil and water supply. Iodine was found to be necessary to the functioning of the thyroid gland in its production of the hormone thyroxin, the absence of which can cause cretinism.

The addition of iodine to table salt resulted in reducing mental retardation caused by endemic cretinism to near zero. It also led to the preventive and therapeutic use of extract of thyroxin in the treatment of myxoedema or hypothyroidism from other causes (Kanner, 1957).

The incidence of Down's syndrome is well-documented. It has been identified with a specific chromosomal abnormality which occurs most frequently as an unpredictable non-disjunction of autosome 21, but infrequently also as the Mendelian transmission of a translocated portion of autosome 21. The former type is definitely related to maternal age, occurring at about .33 per thousand live births to mothers under age 29 but rising sharply after age 35 to a rate of about 25 per thousand to women over age 45.

Overall, the incidence of Down's syndrome is 1 in 600 to 700 live births, with over half occurring to women over 35 (Begab, 1974). The overall incidence of gross chromosomal malformation of children born to women over 35 is 1 to 2 percent (Lubs and Ruddle, 1970; Begab, 1974). The existence of the condition is detectable by amniocentesis (analysis of a sample of amniotic fluid) during pregnancy.

This knowledge creates the possibility of

reducing the incidence of Down's syndrome substantially by: a) limiting pregnancy after age 35; b) detecting the transmissable karyotype of translocation in either the male or female and limiting reproduction; c) identifying the condition early in gestation and terminating pregnancy.

A third example of incidence is more problematic, but nevertheless significant. From prevalence studies, it is known that mild retardation is more frequently found in families of low socio-economic status, especially in families in which the mother is mildly retarded. Heber and others have determined that the incidence of retardation in such families can be reduced by early intervention in providing stimulation to the child and home assistance to the mother.

These examples are sufficient to illustrate the values of pursuing the study of incidence to identifiable causes or correlative conditions as a means of identifying preventive measures (see Stein and Susser, 1974; Begab, 1974). Further discussion of currently known preventive measures appear in later chapters on prevention.

Prevalence

The principal problems of obtaining reliable prevalence estimates relate to definitions, criteria and administrative procedures on the one hand, and to the absence of uniform and centralized data collection, on the other. The former problems are gradually becoming resolved. The latter requires vigorous and sustained efforts by Federal and State governments to establish an effective data bank.

Prevalence is a product of cumulative incidence modified by loss. Loss may be the result of death or cure or unaccounted disappearance. Whereas measures of incidence are important to the problem of prevention, measures of prevalence are important to the provision of service resources. As prevention requires differential classification by identifiable cause, so service provision requires differential classification by types of need.

Overall estimates of prevalence of mental retardation have been made by two methods: by empirical surveys and by selection of a cut-off point on a Gaussian curve for the distribution of intelligence scores. The latter has led to a widely used estimate of 3%, ambiguously referring to either incidence or prevalence. This would correspond to an IQ level of approximately 70 and is, in fact, an average general prevalence found in some surveys of children (Conley, 1973; Birch et al, 1970).

However, it possible to select a 9% cut-off at about IQ 80 or 16% at IQ 85, the 1961 AAMD criterion. All surveys, however, show that mental retardation does not represent a simple portion of the lower tail on a general Gaussian curve. It is far from being normally distributed, varying widely by age, by socio-economic and ethnic factors. The use of an IQ cut-off alone also assumes a one-dimensional definition of mental retardation, contrary to the AAMD formula and other leading authorities (Tarjan, 1973; Mercer, 1973).

Tarjan (1973, p. 370) points out that the estimate of 3% prevalence, or 6 million persons in the United States, makes four dubious assumptions: "a) the diagnosis of mental retardation is based essentially on an IQ below 70; b) mental retardation is identified in infancy; c) the diagnosis does not change; and d) the mortality of retarded individuals is similar to that of the general population." The first assumption ignores the adaptive behavior component; the second holds only for a small portion, nearly always organically and severely impaired; the third holds only as a generality for those of IQ below 55, and the fourth holds only for the mildly retarded.

As a statement of potential incidence, Tarjan (1973) is probably quite conservative in estimating that 3% of all infants who survive birth will at some time in their lives be identified as mentally retarded in some context—most probably in the public schools.

Epidemiological surveys conducted in various parts of the United States and abroad show comparable prevalence rates for the more seriously retarded—i.e., moderate, severe and profound levels on the AAMD classifications or IQ below 50. Fifteen such studies converge on an average rate of approximately .46% or 4.6 cases per thousand population (Stein and Susser, 1974). These surveys generally covered ages roughly 10 to 20, obscuring the high mortality rate in early childhood. When the surveys are divided between general and rural populations, the three rural studies average at more than double the general rate, or 9.84 per thousand, while the remaining twelve cluster quite closely around 3.6.

Penrose (1963) suggests that prevalence of malformation predictive of profound retardation at birth might be as much as 1 percent, Conley (1973) suggests 1.5 to 1.7 percent, including severe and moderate levels. The rate among prematurely born infants is much higher than among full-term babies. The rate among lower-class nonwhites is higher than among middle-class whites, but the differences are not so striking as is the case in mild retardation levels. Higher rates of prematurity, higher health risk and inferior maternal and child health care could account for the difference at the more severe levels.

In any case, the presumption of actual prevalence of the severe forms of defect predictive of mental retardation would be highest at birth, declining rapidly by mortality to a relatively low rate of .2% in adult life.

Prevalence rates of the severely retarded have been affected by a number of tendencies in the past 20 years. On the one hand, modern medicine has made enormous strides in its ability to preserve life. Infant mortality rates have fallen markedly; survival of prematures at progressively younger ages has become possible, with correspondingly increased risk of developmental damage; recovery from infectious diseases by use of antibiotics has become commonplace. Consequently, along with other infants and young children, severely and profoundly retarded children now have a better chance of prolonged survival.

On the other hand, improved health care, especially for mothers at risk, immunization, protection from radiation exposure, improved obstetrics, control of Rh isoimmunization and other measures have prevented the occurrence of some abnormalities and reduced the complications which formerly added to the incidence and prevalence of retardation. New hazards appear, however, in environmental toxic substances, strains of microorganisms more resistant to antibiotics, new addictive and nonaddictive drugs, new sources of radiation, environmental stress, all of which are potential producers of biological damage and mental retardation (Begab, 1974).

On balance, it is possible that incidence of severe retardation is falling while prevalence is continuing to rise.

The high birth rate of the post World War II period produced a record number of severely retarded children who are surviving longer than ever before. The future, envisioning more control of the causes with a lower birth rate more limited to optimal conditions of reproduction may in time yield lower prevalence rates of the moderate, severely and profound retarded. Currently, a very conservative estimate of their number in the United States is approximately 500,000 (Tarjan, et al, 1973) but may actually be nearer a .3% level or 660,000 surviving beyond the first year of life.

The prevalence of mild retardation is quite a different matter. Where the severely retarded show a declining prevalence by age, based wholly on mortality, the mildly retarded show a sharply peaked prevalence in the school years (6–19) and a rapid falling off in the adult years. This phenomenon cannot be a product of mortality, because the mildly retarded have shown longevity very nearly that of the general population. There are two possible alternatives, both of which may be the case. Large numbers remain retarded but cease to be the objects of attention; or they in fact cease to be retarded. In any case, no survey has yet found prevalence rates of mild retardation remotely approaching a constant across ages, such as would be expected on the assumption of unchanged relative mental status. Tarjan suggests that the rate of 3% traditionally projected as a constant across all ages, actually holds only for the school-age, with rated prevalence in selected age groups of .25% in the 0–5 group, 3.0% from 9–16, .4% from 20 to 24, sinking to .2% in the population over 25; the overall prevalence being approximately 1% (Tarjan, et al, 1973, p. 370). This would yield a total of approximately 2.2 million retarded persons in the United States, as against 6.6 million if an overall 3% is assumed.

In studies of the Riverside, California, population, Mercer (1974) showed that the prevalence and social distribution of mild mental retardation differed markedly according to the definition and methods of identification employed. She compared the application of a "social system" definition ("mental retardate" is an achieved status, and mental retardation is the role associated with the status) with a "clinical" definition (mental retardation is an individual pathology with characteristic symptoms which can be identified by standard diagnostic procedures).

It was found that the use of a one-dimensional clinical definition (IQ less than 69) yielded an overall rate of 2.14% retarded, with Blacks showing a rate 10 times and Mexican-Americans 34 times the rate of Anglos. When a two-dimensional definition is used (IQ less than 69 *plus* deficient adaptive score) the overall rate shrank to .9% which is the "clinical" rate predicted by Tarjan. The distribution now showed Blacks approximately at the same rate as Anglos, but Mexican-Americans still 15 times greater. When pluralistic, culturally adjusted norms were used for both IQ and adaptive behavior, the overall rate reduced still further to .54% but the total shrinkage in this case was accounted for in the Mexican-American group where sociocultural nonmodality (a cultural pattern distinctly different from the predominant mode) and bilingual background were most prominent. Furthermore, when higher criteria for IQ and adaptive behavior were used, the disadvantage to both Blacks and Mexican-Americans, as compared with Anglos, was markedly increased.

The social distribution of mild mental retardation has been found by all investigators to be inversely related to socio-economic status. It is, according to Conley (1973) 13 times more prevalent among poor than among middle and upper income groups and found most frequently among rural, isolated or ghetto populations. Controversy persists concerning the contribution of constitutional and social learning factors to this distribution, but it is a question of the relative wieght rather than an exclusive alternative. No one doubts the multiple effects of environmental deprivation on both physical and psychological development. Nor is there much doubt that social learning enables the great majority of those with mild intellectual limitations to assume normal social roles in adult life. It is evident that what might appear to be a manifestation of the normal distribution of polygenic general intelligence is really a complex product in which the genetic component is only one among many factors yielding varying degrees and rates of retarded behavior, among varying populations at varying ages.

There is little point, then, in arguing who is "really" retarded. There is great point in determining who is in need of developmental and supportive assistance in achieving a reasonably adequate adult life, in determining the relationships between identifiable characteristics and the kinds of services that will be profitable, and in employing terminology that will aid rather than obscure these relationships. A critical issue is the degree to which cultural pluralism is reflected in the educational process.

The classification suggested by Mercer (1973) involves a four-dimensional matrix in which potentially handicapping conditions, including mental retardation defined in either "clinical" or "social system" terms, may be identified:

a) The dimension of *intellectual functioning,* measurable on a continuous scale represented by IQ. On this scale, following the 1973 AAMD standard, an IQ of 69 or less is regarded as potentially handicapping and is one clinically defining characteristic of mental retardation. Mercer terms the person with *only* this dimension of disability as *quasi-retarded.* Ordinarily this will be reflected in learning difficulties in the school setting and justifies individually prescriptive educational assistance.

b) The dimension of *adaptive behavior,* measurable on a developmental scale of behavioral controls accommodating the person to his environment. On this dimension a person falling substantially below age norms (perhaps in the lowest 3% of a normative distribution) is regarded as potentially handicapped. This constitutes a second clinically defining characteristic of mental retardation of the 1973 AAMD standard. Mercer terms the person who

has *only* this dimension of disability as *behaviorally maladjusted,* but she identifies the person with disability in both a) and b) as *clinically mentally retarded,* requiring services in both school and non-school settings.

c) The dimension of *physical constitution,* describable in terms of the health or pathology of the various organ systems of the body. While not a defining characteristic of mental retardation, physical impairment may be in itself potentially handicapping and may be the cause of or magnify the handicapping limitations of a) and b). The probability of organic impairments being present increases with the severity of mental retardation, from 3% at mild retardation levels to 78% at moderate levels and 95% at severe and profound levels (Conley, 1973, pp. 46–7). Individuals characterized by only c) may be termed generically as *physically impaired,* and in combination with a) and b) as *organic mentally retarded.* The term "multiply handicapped" is commonly used, but this would apply equally to persons with more than one substantial physical impairment.

d) *Sociocultural modality* is a fourth dimension which is distinguishable from the other three. It refers to the extent to which sociocultural variables of family background conform or do not conform to the modal culture in which the individual is assessed. When the family background is substantially non-modal, in this sense, the individual may be potentially handicapped in relation to the prevailing cultural expectations because of lack of opportunity for the appropriate learning. Such a person may be termed *culturally disadvantaged.* Mercer found that non-modality yielded effects which, to the dominant culture, appeared as low IQ, low adaptive behavior, or both when measured by the norms of the dominant culture. Utilizing a pluralistic model of mental retardation, sensitive to socio-cultural differences, Mercer found a substantial reduction in the prevalence of mental retardation in the Mexican-American as compared to the Anglo population of Riverside. Throughout the investigation, the Anglo sample yielded a constant rate of 4.4 per thousand identified as mentally retarded (i.e. no Anglos in this sample were judged either quasi-retarded or non-modal culturally). The Mexican-

American population yielded the following succession of rates per 1,000:

 a) One dimensional—only standard IQ norms, 149.0

 b) Two dimensional—standard IQ + standard adaptive behavior norms, 60.0

 c) Partial pluralistic two dimensional—standard IQ, pluralistic adaptive behavior norms, 30.4

 d) Pluralistic two dimensional—pluralistic norms for both IQ and adaptive behavior, 15.3

(Mercer, 1973, pp. 235–254)

The residual differences between the rate of 4.4 for Anglos and the 15.3 rate for culturally adapted assessment of Mexican-Americans may be attributable to the pervasive effects of their bilingual status.

Granted that Mercer's research is based on a single local population sampling and is a first approach to a "social systems" definition of mental retardation, it suggests the need for much more highly refined procedures in the definition and epidemiology of mental retardation as a basis for the adequate and appropriate delivery of developmental and supportive services where they are needed.

There is complete agreement that it is impossible, at our present state of knowledge, to determine accurately either the incidence or the prevalence of mental retardation. There is far less agreement on what we can do to remedy this situation. Among the most urgent issues in classification:

1. **Definition.** The formulation adopted by the American Association on Mental Deficiency involving two-dimensional deficit in the level of behavioral performance unquestionably is responsive to many problems arising from older definitions. But a number of issues remain:

 a) The two dimensions are not independent, but are, in fact, highly correlated, the degree of correlation being related to severity of deficit, suggesting the distinction of intellectual and adaptive measures has not been sufficiently refined. In practice, more reliance is frequently placed on IQ measures than on measures of adaptation or other bases of clinical judgment.

 b) The cultural contamination of standardized tests as currently used makes their findings suspect. Mercer and others require a corrective for cultural insensitivity of the instruments employed.

 c) The use of a global IQ measure which may be adequate for epidemiological purposes obscures the complexity of intellectual functioning and the variability of individual profiles which is the basis of service provision. Global IQ measures are rapidly losing favor among professional pro-

viders of service but are maintained for administrative convenience and ease of determination.

 d) Differences in the conditions associated with mild retardation as compared to the more severe forms in terms of organicity, comprehensiveness of impairment, resistance to modification, relatedness to cultural norms, etc., suggest to some that the two types are sufficiently different as to require separate classification, probably based on organic (or presumed organic) versus psychosocial etiology.

2. **Services.** Since the instruments for the measurement of intelligence and adaptive behavior are scalar, with continuous variation on both sides of central norms, the relationship between a specific level of deficit and the need for specific types of service and treatment may be highly artificial. This appears to be the central question underlying the controversy over the criterion level in the AAMD definition which now excludes persons with IQs from 70 to 85 who formerly were included. The fact that relatively few scoring above 69 IQ manifest significant deficits in adaptive behavior may miss the point. Adaptive behavior may be quite specific and situational, especially where culture modality may also be in question. The real issue is to determine individual need, which cannot be derived from the IQ or adaptive behavior. This issue has been exacerbated by legislation which requires categorical classification as a condition of eligibility for service.

3. **Labeling.** Titles are necessary for any scientific system of classification, and may be useful for certain administrative purposes; but their use in human service systems is a different matter. The attachment of a label to a species of plant or a type of rock makes no difference to the plant or the rock. The label assigned to classify a human being does make a difference. To label a person mentally retarded has consequences of a psychological nature if the person is cognizant of it and can assign a meaning to it; it has consequences of a social nature insofar as other persons assign meaning and respond in terms of that meaning. This is especially the case with the label of "mentally retarded" because all terms associated with deficiency of intelligence are, in our culture, highly charged with negative values.

There have been many attempts to use systems of intellect classification as a means of adapting school and other programs to individual differences without making those differences appear invidious. These have not been entirely successful because value systems, even for children, tend to filter through the most subtle of euphemistic terminology.

This is a difficult issue to resolve. Success is possible only if: a) classification for epidemiological purposes is entirely separated from need-evaluation for purposes of social grouping and prescriptive treatment, b) all treatment is person-centered rather than system-centered, c) cultural value systems are recognized and respected, and d) eligibility for categorical assistance is based, not on global statistical criteria, but on the individual's need.

4. **Recording, Registering and Information Control** (corollary to labeling). Obviously, the best data base for the epidemiologist would be a computerized data bank including all information on every case. This has, in effect, been advocated since Samuel Howe's first attempt to catalogue the "idiotic" population of Massachusetts in 1848, long before modern systems of information storage and retrieval were dreamed of. However, rights of privacy and confidentiality have become a critical issue. The problem is one of reconciling the needs of the service delivery system and the individual recipient, so that he will neither be "lost" as an anonymous number nor stigmatized for having his needs recognized.

5. **"Negativism."** The nature of retardation lends itself to definition and assessment in the negative terms of deficit from desirable norms. The individual person, however, is not made up of deficits but of asset characteristics, however meager or distorted some of them may be. All treatment rests on the positive capacity of the person to respond, whether physiologically or psychologically. The issue of negatively versus positively defined traits and classifications is a basic one between the purposes of epidemiology and the purposes of service assistance.

Who are the people who are mentally retarded? They are individuals whose assets for effective living in their cultural and physical environments are insufficient without assistance. The screen by which they are brought into view to be identified and counted is composed of a mesh of intellectual and adaptive behavior norms. But the screen is a somewhat crude and abrasive instrument and requires to be refined and softened by concern for the individuals it exposes.

How many mentally retarded people are there? The loss of potential for normal development and even survival affects a high proportion of those who are conceived, and probably 3% of those who survive birth. In addition to those hundreds of thousands who are not well-born, there are millions who are not well-nurtured by the world in which they live. How we sort out these millions, how many will be called "mentally retarded" will depend on our definitions and our perceptions of need. The roots of these needs are not yet under control, nor have we sufficiently provided for their assuagement.

PLATE I

Sketch from the colored illustration of the simplest picture in the series, the demonstration picture, with the inserts which particularly relate to this picture. Of course only one is quite correct, but the others can be inserted with some show of reasonableness.

Educating the twenty-four hour retarded child

Recent court decisions and legislative actions have overturned our school systems' long-standing privilege of denying public education to severely handicapped children. While this must certainly be viewed as a significant victory in the fight for the rights of the individual, the "zero-reject" movement has undeniably subjected the educational community to the brunt of new parental, legal and legislative pressures. Educational administrators and professionals are increasingly faced with new, and often unanticipated issues affecting the education of severely or profoundly retarded students within the public school system. In many instances, both educators and parents alike have been unprepared to cope with this sudden shift in responsibility.

The National Association for Retarded Citizens, the Bureau of Education for the Handicapped and many other interested organizations and individuals share this concern, and seek answers to the problem of fulfilling the public school educational needs of severely and profoundly retarded students. In the spring of 1975, over 700 persons from 46 states gathered in New Orleans, Louisiana. Participants of the conference, entitled "Educating the 24-Hour Retarded Child," included state education agency personnel, program administrators, teachers, teacher trainers, university students, and many others. Some came to share their experience regarding current educational programs for severely handicapped persons. Others sought knowledge which might help them meet the challenge of this new concept. Some participants questioned the feasibility of public education for the markedly retarded student — and wanted answers. All felt that changes must be made on the part of educational service agencies in order to meet their new responsibilities of educating *all* children.

This conference brought together for the first time those persons responsible for monitoring and delivering services to severely and profoundly mentally retarded individuals. NARC believes that the success of the gathering was a meaningful step in assuring appropriate public school educational services for severely and profoundly retarded children.

From the NARC Research and Demonstration Insititute, New Orleans, 1975.

"We are dealing with the most severely handicapped members of the human race—individuals whose nervous systems have been seriously damaged, or never developed properly. The severely and profoundly retarded include approximately the lowest 5% of the retarded population. More than 99% of all persons learn more easily than they do. Many have IQs that may be termed 'unmeasurable.'
"When these children enter school they may exhibit a wide variety of social and developmental handicaps. Still, all of these children are human beings—all have a right to learn, to develop and to be treated as individuals."

Dr. Phillip Roos
Executive Director
National Association for
Retarded Citizens

The conference opened on the evening of March 31 to a standing-room-only crowd in the International Ballroom of the Fairmont Hotel. Opening remarks were given by Dr. Walter J. Cegelka, Chairman of the NARC Education Subcommittee. Dr. Philip Roos, Executive Director of the Association, then challenged conference participants to meet the needs of the future, and pointed out that in a land where human rights are held in high esteem, our actions have not always kept pace with our ideals.

Dr. Roos noted that while social justice has taken giant strides within this century, the basic human and legal rights of countless thousands of our citizens have been violated. They have been denied access to desperately needed resources, and subjected to dehumanizing practices — practices sanctioned on the assumption that there are degrees of humanness, and that only the "fully human" are entitled to participate in society — that deviations from cultural norms are valid grounds for rejection and isolation.

Dr. Roos noted that although recent legislation, federal regulations and court decisions have reaffirmed the basic premise of our national philosophy, we should not delude ourselves into the belief that new laws will work magic — that severely and profoundly retarded persons' biological limitations are inconsequential. We

cannot assume that all people can develop into so-called "normal" human beings if only presented with the proper environment. Yet, much can be done to help these severely handicapped individuals. Impressive programs are now underway. Research has documented the value of new procedures. Techniques are now available which have demonstrated effectiveness. But we are still in the dark ages when it comes to understanding the human mind. We have, however, taken the first few steps in what promises to be a long and rewarding journey.

What can be done to help severely and profoundly retarded individuals? Despite the serious nature of these students' handicaps, Dr. Sidney Bijou of the University of Illinois gave conference participants cause for optimism in his discussion of the behavioral approach and its applications to the educational problems of mentally retarded students. Behavioral techniques, based on operant conditioning, have been applied to the teaching of retarded persons at all levels for just over 15 years, and at present are considered by many ranking educators to be the approach with the greatest potential.

Many problems have resulted from misunderstandings about the nature of this approach. Operant conditioning is the strengthening of "purposive" behavior, and is vastly different from the

"The application of behavior principles to the teaching of retarded children is not another educational fad, and those who might stand around patiently waiting for it to pass will be disappointed. Since it is the end product of 50 years of experimental research and theory construction, it is likely that with continued support of basic and applied research, it will become even more effective."

Dr. Sidney W. Bijou
Member, NARC Research Committee
Professor of Psychology
University of Illinois, Champaign

conditioning methods which shocked the public in *Brave New World*, *1984*, *The Manchurian Candidate*, and *Clockwork Orange*. Basically, behavioral analysis consists of determining specifically what skill we want a child to learn, dividing that skill into its components and systematically reinforcing the desired behavior.

The applied behavioral analysis format for teaching the severely and profoundly retarded child can be implemented in both the classroom and home setting. In either case, success depends largely upon teacher training, commitment and administrative support. Teachers must abandon their traditional concepts of curriculum if they are to be successful with severely and profoundly retarded students. They must be trained to deal with a whole range of behaviors that have rarely been the concern of the public schools. The traditional three R's are simply not enough here. Teachers must be prepared to help their students learn to survive in the world from the moment they wake up in the morning until they go to bed at night.

Active parent participation is more than an ingredient in this approach — it is a *must*. Without it, there is little hope that behaviors acquired in the classroom will be maintained.

profoundly retarded children. This agency has established as a broad goal the provision of equal educational opportunities for all handicapped children. With respect to severely handicapped individuals, the Bureau's aim is to enable this group to become as independent as possible, thereby re-

ducing their requirements for institutional care and providing opportunity for self-development.

Establishing such services is a big job. Mr. Ed Wilson, a Program Specialist with the Bureau, reminded conference participants that an estimated one million severely handicapped children are now totally excluded from the educational system, while at least another 300,000 are not receiving adequate services. There are a number of reasons why: a lack of experienced personnel . . . a general void of appropriate curricula and training programs . . . a scarcity of specialized materials and equipment, and a general lack of concern, in many quarters, for the needs of such persons.

Certainly, providing proper educational services for all retarded children is one of the most vital issues in the field of mental retardation. At the 1975 New Orleans Conference, Dr. Edwin W. Martin, Acting Deputy Director of Education, Bureau of Education for the Handicapped, pointed out that we are witnessing a growing sense of national commitment in this area. This commitment is reflected in part by the emphasis Commissioner Bell has placed on programs for all handicapped persons and in part by the Bureau's high priority on funding for severely handicapped students.

Dr. Martin emphasized the Bureau's role in the implementation of a new provision of the Education of the Handicapped Act which requires the states to make a commitment to educating the more severely handicapped children. He noted that Congress has charged

"As a part of our nation's growing concern for the handicapped, we have seen the Congress enact legislation increasingly based on a commitment to children. We have also seen the Judicial Branch representing the rights of handicapped children in a more vigorous way. This concern has not been limited, of course, to federal government bodies. There has been a tremendous amount of interest--perhaps more than in any other area--expressed by the states themselves.

Dr. Edwin W. Martin
Deputy Commissioner of Education
Bureau of Education for the
 Handicapped
U.S Office of Education

BEH with the responsibility of distributing funds with the priority upon unserved children.

The Bureau of Education for the Handicapped is perhaps one of the strongest forces behind the implementation of legislation and the provision of programs beneficial to severely and

It is clear that institutions of higher education must drastically redefine their roles if they intend to provide quality personnel for instructing handicapped children. The Bureau's Dr. Edward Sontag noted that it is no longer enough for universities to serve as predominantly "preservice delivery systems." Equal emphasis must be placed upon inservice, staff development, and preservice training. Universities must also accept the responsibility for retraining those professionals already in their employ.

It is a rare school system that provides comprehensive programs for severely retarded, severely emotionally disturbed, and multiply handicapped students. While severely handicapped students, as a general group, present no more administrative problems than any other students, they do bring to bear problems that are more pervasive, intense—and more expensive to solve. Most school systems now have little experience in matters such as needed medical services, transportation, affiliations with non-school agencies, etc.

There are a number of areas of concern in the educational field in regard to severely retarded people. Basic to the needs of this population is the provision of continuous educational op-

portunities. Every effort must be made to provide developmental intervention services for severely handicapped individuals of all ages.

Much can be done within the public school system to assure that severely retarded students receive the educational opportunities they deserve. Essential, however, to the students' successful participation in any such program is parental involvement throughout the educative process. Frances Bicknell of the Wisconsin Association for Retarded Citizens reminded conference participants that parents of retarded children have a proud record of accomplishment in this area. They have helped administer day care and educational centers for their children who were excluded from public schools, and have participated in every activity from janitorial duties to the drafting of successful legislation. Now, however, parental roles are changing, and the emphasis should be on cooperative efforts with educators in assuring adequate educational services.

Dr. Luke S. Watson, President of Behavior Modification Technology, Inc., pointed out that parents can be invaluable allies in the educative process, and noted that there is impressive evidence that programs employing parents as behavior modification technicians have the potential to provide an economical, effective alternative to existing clinical intervention techniques.

Inherent in the provision of adequate opportunities for severely

"If we are truly to achieve our goals in this field, we must dedicate ourselves to some basic—but vital—operating premises. We must promote community understanding of the fact that severely and profoundy handicapped children can, and should be served in the public school sector; that they can be integrated into many regular school activities; and that they are capable of learning beyond our current expectations. We must understand that parental participation is essential to expanding successful intervention strategies for severely handicapped children."

Dr. Edward Sontag, Chief
Cognitive and Affective Branch
Division of Personnel Preparatio
Bureau of Education for the
 Handicapped
U.S. Office of Education

and profoundly retarded persons are services and needs directly related to the actual educational process. The expense of such programs is a problem that must be faced — and solved — by the public in general, and the school systems concerned, in particular. Dr. Jean McGrew of the Madison, Wisconsin Public Schools, addressed these problems at the New Orleans meeting, stressing that while legislatures have mandated that school systems provide adequate programs for all severely and profoundly handicapped students, they have mandated responsibility without providing for the actual financial support itself. Most school districts, then, must reallocate finances that are already stretched to the limit to provide such programs. McGrew reminded participants that while conferences such as the New Orleans meeting provide good opportunities for special education professionals to share mutual concerns, it is imperative that dialogue be established with persons who have administrative control over the selection of programs for funding. He stressed the importance of establishing close cooperation with those in the position of making decisions within the public schools, including especially school board members.

Another important consideration in the educative process is the environment of the retarded student. George Gray of the New York Department of Mental Hygiene noted that many educational facilities exhibit restrictive environments for handicapped children, and pointed out that these children should, ideally, be placed where they can obtain the best education, at the least distance from mainstream society. Society should be aware of the condition, problems and potentials of such children — and this awareness is not enhanced by hiding them from public view.

Progress is evident in the area of environmental concern for the severely and profoundly retarded. The mutual use of space shared by special education and regular instruction has influenced the origin of a new type of school specially designed to integrate handicapped and non-handicapped students. Open school and environmental play complexes are providing rich, new worlds of stimulation and opportunity to support the efforts of those responsible for teaching the severely retarded student.

Concern for a proper teaching curriculum for severely handicapped students has prompted a number of efforts to develop sound, workable guidelines. Dr. Norris Haring of the University of Washington noted the importance of coordinating these efforts and evolving a developmental curriculum with a valid theoretical rationale and a common content base throughout the many levels of development. Such a curriculum could remain in a state of continuous development for some time, allowing for periodic modification or refinement based on the performance records of a

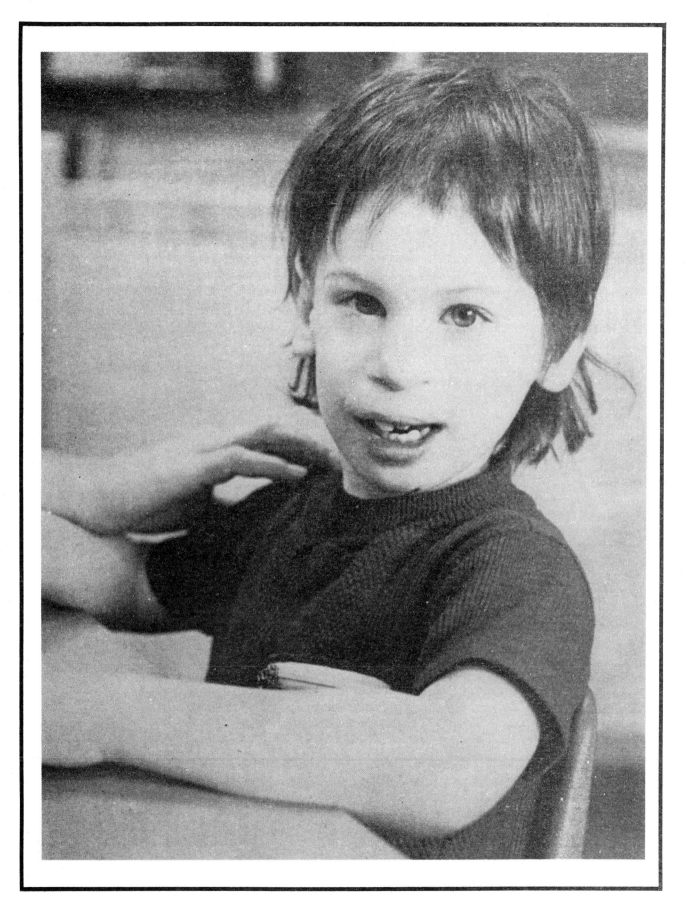

"We believe that the utilization of data on child development is the most practical basis for arriving at uniform guidelines for teaching the typical infant and child. Through developmental pinpoints, we can establish a child's exact place in the sequence of skills development, and provide programming interventions that match the child's instructional needs."

Dr. Norris G. Haring, Director
Child Development and Mental
  Retardation Center
Experimental Education Unit
University of Washington, Seattle

number of handicapped children.

As Haring pointed out, time must not be consumed teaching responses, skills and facts that are not essential to increasing the independence of the severely handicapped child. This concern was reiterated by Dr. Lou Brown of the University of Wisconsin, who noted that it is vital that public schools prepare severely handicapped students to function as independently as possible socially, vocationally and personally in the least restricting post-school environment. He further stated that preparing students to function in large residential institutions, or for fostering or maintaining the development of environments that unduly shelter or restrict the individual cannot be justified.

Because of limited educational opportunities in the past, and the almost inevitable placement of severely and profoundly retarded citizens in large institutions, it might once have been acceptable to teach this population to "walk in line," or "make pot holders," with little concern for *why* such skills were taught. Now, though, severely handicapped students will be enrolled in public school programs for as long as twenty-one years. Longitudinal public education, coupled with the goals of the deinstitutionalization and child advocacy movements, compel us to *justify* the teaching of any specific skill.

Indeed, increased understanding · of the components of sound public school educational services was one of the goals of the "Educating the 24-Hour Retarded Child" Conference. Hopefully, through the collective efforts of many persons from diverse orien-

tations and backgrounds, comprehensive, longitudinal and quality educational services *can* be generated, and substantial developmental changes will result in both the functioning levels and ultimate lifestyles of those citizens who—for the moment, at least — are referred to as severely handicapped.

Dr. Cecil Colwell of the Northwest Louisiana State School pointed out the need for changing our way of thinking about teaching the retarded individual, noting that we have, for some years, actively pursued a self-contradictory course in dealing with mentally retarded persons. Through words and deeds, we have said that the profoundly retarded *cannot* be trained. At the same time, we have instructed our attendants in residential institutions to vigorously carry out training in environments so sterile that we knew little progress would be made.

Recently, however, we have begun to re-examine our concepts and have found we have more resources than we thought we did. Through the use of techniques based on the stimuli-response-reinforcement model, many programs have developed which have demonstrated success in educating the severely and profoundly retarded person to act and behave in a more normal fashion.

Establishing educational programs for the severely and profoundly retarded in public schools is, of course, only one aspect of the problem. Dr. Charles Galloway of the Eastern Nebraska Community Office of Retardation, informed conference participants of some of the problems of providing educational services in non-public school settings. While such services are, necessarily, critical to meeting the current needs of these students, we should remember that the very existence of education in non-public settings represents a community-wide compromise when these programs parallel public services available to most children or adults in the community. Agencies now providing such services should consider their purposes carefully, and examine the degree to which they might be supporting an exclusionary and isolationist community policy toward a segment of the population.

While conference participants were vitally aware of the need for proper educational programming for the severely and profoundly retarded student, they were also cognizant of the many problems inherent in turning "good intentions" into practical, working programs. One of the most vital ingredients to a successful program is a vast reservoir of properly trained teachers. Unfortunately, we are critically short of such talent. Now that we have established new legislation to assure the rights of severely and profoundly handicapped individuals, we must turn those rights into active, worthwhile programs. Can we do it? Will the net effect of our efforts be to transport more children faster to participate in ineffective instruction? We may be able to create instant authority for our actions through court or legislative mandates, but we cannot create instant teachers or programs to carry out that authority. We can't assume that needs will be fulfilled simply because there is social agreement that such needs exist.

Dr. Edward L. Meyen of the University of Kansas pointed out that we have more colleges and universities *preparing* to train personnel to teach the severely and profoundly handicapped than we have currently established programs.

We must not repeat our history of twenty years ago, when it seemed quite proper for every teachers college in the country to train special class teachers for the mildly mentally retarded student.

What, then, is the answer? The typical special education faculty is not oriented toward the training strategies necessary to prepare teaching personnel for the severely and profoundly retarded. University funding for such activities is difficult to come by. Most of our present programs are supported through federal funding. Without that funding, any program continuation becomes speculative at best.

Possible answers to these problems are on the horizon. One potential solution is a network of regional training centers to provide for area recruitment and better utilization of available resources.

Additionally, while there are virtually no certification programs for teachers of the severely and profoundly retarded, there *are* highly competent non-credentialed teachers who *have* had extensive and successful experience in private non-profit agency classes and other non-public school facilities. Dr. James Tawney of the University of Kentucky touched upon this subject at the conference, and urged development of a performance-based certification program which would enable these teachers to continue working with children — a standard that would also enable the exclusion of inept teachers from the classroom. Certification, he noted, should be based on proof of positive change in child performance. It stands to reason that a competency based model may well be more appropriate for training teachers of severely and profoundly handicapped pupils than for any other target population of learners.

What skills does a teacher need to teach the severely and profoundly retarded individual — and what are the most effective methods of utilizing these skills? Dr. Lou Brown pointed out

"The rapid expansion of special education programs during the past ten years is a poor predictor of the future in terms of adding additional training programs today. It is difficult to establish new courses, let alone new programs. The changing climate in higher education has come at a time when departments of special education are experiencing large-scale demands for personnel---and finite funds."

Dr. Edward L. Meyen, Chairman
Department of Special Education
University of Kansas, Lawrence

that one of the more crucial differences between teaching normal or mildly handicapped students and severely retarded students is the degree of precision required when *presenting* instructional content.

The skills required and fostered by a task analysis orientation seem ideally suited for teachers in this field. Through this discipline, such initially nebulous objectives as teaching a value, an appreciation, an attitude, a skill, a concept, an understanding, a subtlety or a feeling *can* be accomplished with severely handicapped students. Realistic objectives are established, and instruction is tailored to individual functioning levels — greatly facilitating the development of more effective and efficient classroom programming.

Dr. Alice Hayden of the University of Washington noted that teachers must learn how to make accurate assessments of child performance based on systematic observation. They have an excellent vantage point for watching a child over an extended period of time, in a natural setting. By learning to alert themselves to those handicapping conditions that develop slowly and cumulatively, they can take steps to remediate them early — and can also adjust curriculum needs accordingly.

As Dr. Frances Connor of Columbia University stated in New Orleans, severely and multiply handicapped children are individuals. Therefore, teachers of these students must develop the knowledge and skill to enable them to know how their pupils function at different stages of development, how they learn best, how their environment can be modified to promote learning, and how to evaluate the effectiveness of the teaching process.

Dr. Burton Blatt summed up the feelings of conference participants when he noted that each human being has unduplicatable value. That value is not bound to his educability, but to his intrinsic and inalienable right to be respected — because he *is* a human being. We do not always recognize, or acknowledge that right. During a person's life he struggles to realize his gifts, while society seeks to trap him, tame him and standardize him to fit society's picture of itself. Sometimes, though, for better or for worse, we come across people who will *not* be molded. They cause us problems, yet they are our major investment in the future. And it has always been society's dilemma to decide who should be molded and controlled, and who should be free as the wind.

Dr. Blatt further pointed out that one irony of our culture is that we revere life but disdain freedom. In our zeal to protect the weak, the aged and the handicapped, we segregate, stigmatize and make pariahs out of whole legions of people. We build institutions to incarcerate the blind and the retarded. And when these "different" people are out of sight and out of mind, we not only shut the door against their chance to "see" and understand us, we preclude any possibility that *we* will ever see and understand them.

"We encourage freedom and individuality, while we weed out those who appear to be dangerous and maladaptive--and pray that serious blunders have not been perpetrated in the name of society. Children must always exemplify humanity's universal and continuing enthusiasm for a better future. If we fail with children, we fail with everything."

Dr. Burton Blatt, Director
Division of Special Education
and Rehabilitation
Syracuse University
Syracuse, New York

The concept that all people are entitled to freedom under a just law has bloodied the soil of many nations. Sometimes the concept falters — sometimes it takes a step forward. But the idea of freedom, individuality, human values and human resources continues to intrude upon the public consciousness, crying for legitimacy and support. Hopefully, those people who gathered in New Orleans in the spring of 1975 will play an important part in upholding and forwarding at least one aspect of that idea.

In Retrospect...

Public school curricula must be designed to accommodate the special learning needs of severely and profoundly retarded students.

Public school services should be viewed as only one component in an overall community effort to provide appropriate life-long services for severely and profoundly handicapped individuals.

Efforts to establish programs which provide parents with the necessary skills and knowledge to become effectively involved in educational programming should be promoted.

Educational services for severely handicapped children should be located so as to provide appropriate education in the least restrictive environment possible.

Universities should place as much importance on inservice training and staff development as they presently do on preservice teacher education.

Certification programs should be performance-based to ensure that only the most competent teachers are allowed to work with those students who need the most help.

Educational funds should be redistributed in school programs so that severely handicapped students may receive the quality educational services to which they are entitled.

National commitment should continue to be directed toward providing proper educational services to all handicapped students.

Normalized Interaction with Families of the Mentally Retarded — To Introduce Attitude and Behavior Change in Students in a Professional Discipline

Alexander Hersh
Raymond W. Carlson
David A. Lossino

Research on the impact of education on social work students attitudes and behavior toward mental retardation has been inconclusive. Results offer support for a conclusion suggested by Begab (1970) and Prothero and Ehlers (1974) that knowledge derived through affective experiences has greater impact on attitude formulation than knowledge alone. To extend this line of research, this pilot study was carried out using a short, elective course on developmental disabilities at a school of social work. The focus of the study was a supplementary experience involving one day of interaction with a family with a retarded member.

The Course

The basis for the study was a seven session elective introductory course on developmental disabilities, for example--mental retardation, cerebral palsy, and the epilepsies. The course, which has been offered on five previous occasions has evolved into a carefully shaped experience designed to achieve pre-determined educational objectives suitable to the needs of professionals who will encounter handicapped persons in their future professional work roles (Krishef & Levine, 1968, Hersh & Brown, 1974).

The course outline is as follows:

1. Definitions, causes, categories, classifications, incidence, prevalence, outlook and prognostication.

2. Major trends and social change perspectives—on handicapping disorders; e.g. changing attitudes and values, normalization principle, citizens rights, e.g. to education, treatment, advocacy.

3. Conceptual framework for working with handicapped persons, their families and communities; psychological—social parameters; special needs, characteristics, considerations and approaches.

4. An extensive reading list is provided for required and recommended reading and visual aids are sometimes used; each student is required to write a major paper, focusing on a specific area of learning from the course.

Procedures

1. At the first and seventh session, each student was asked to rank-order his/her preference as prospective professionals for being assigned clients of 10 varying categories, e.g., juvenile delinquent, aged, mentally ill, mentally retarded.

2. At the same session, each student completed a 19-item semantic differential on expectations for mentally retarded vs. normal individuals.

3. Small group structural role-playing was implemented during sessions two and seven. A coded observation form was used to identify the nature of the helping behavior reflected by those playing social work roles and the type of responses of those playing client roles. The results were classified to consider the degree of respect the helping behavior and client response reflected.

4. Subjective discussions of the experimental experience and the research instruments were conducted during the sixth and seventh sessions.

Results

The results for each procedure were as follows:

1. Mental retardation had an average rank of 6.6 for the initial responses for the experimental group and 3.9 for the nonexperimental group. The second testing resulted in an average rank of 3.5 for the experimental group and 3.6 for the nonexperimental ones. In part, the initial differences were related to the nonexperimental group being more experienced with retardation, but the pattern was not consistent. Thus, the results imply an impact in the experimental experience but suggest need for greater clarification of the initial differences.

2. Initially, the tendency was to rank the mentally retarded slightly lower than the normal person. Those objectives with the lowest ratings for the mentally retarded (in contrast to the normal ratings) were dependence, having a physical handicap, being unpredictable, being aimless, being useless, and being untidy—in that order. On the other hand, the mentally retarded were consistently rated higher than normal people on being kind, good, and not dangerous. By the final ratings, differences between the mentally retarded and normal group

were almost nonexistent. Dependence and being physically handicapped were the only items in which the mentally retarded averaged lower Again, those with the experimental experience made a more positive change than those without the visits. Limited or no previous experience with retardation was particularly important in this attitudinal test.

3. A series of changes was identified between the initial and final role play. The social workers became more directive and less subtle in their approach. The clients became less resistive and were less likely to take over the social worker role during the latter session. These results, though, are based on only one initial and one later role-playing experience. Consequently, the results must be viewed cautiously, and comparison of those in the experimental and non-experimental groups is meaningless.

4. The students participating in the experimental visits were enthusiastic about those visits. Several suggested positive change in their respect for these families, in their attitudes toward retardation, and their self-understanding. Only one student had a negative experience resulting from one parent refusing to interact because he mistakenly got the impression the student was studying abnormal psychology. The students recommended the visits be included as a feature of subsequent classes. One student who had not participated in the visits suggested similar changes occurred because of the increased field placement experience with mentally retarded clients.

These initial results must be viewed as tentative considering the small number of students involved and the students' knowledge that they were participating in an experiment. Since the results were supportive, the experiment will be continued. With such replication, additional clarification will be sought, concerning initial variation in scores, the development of self-understanding, the effect of the experimental visits on the role-playing behavior, and the possible effect of knowing the experience is experimental. The focus of the study was an educational innovation involving students visiting families with a developmentally disabled member. The procedure shows promise as a means of effective attitudinal and behavioral change in prospective professionals.

The Experimental Experience

An organization of families with mentally retarded members was asked to seek volunteers who would be willing to spend a day with a social work student. Thirteen families volunteered, and one student was assigned to visit each family. Two of the visits had to be cancelled for pragmatic reasons and one because the family changed its mind. Structuring of the visit was left to the student and family.

Selection of Sample

Students were asked to indicate willingness to participate in the experimental experience. Twenty out of 25 responded positively, with the others listing the extensiveness of previous experience as the reason for not volunteering. The 20 were subdivided into three groups according to amount of previous experience with mentally retarded individuals. Within each subgroup, individuals were randomly assigned to either have or not have the experimental experience. The only exception was that the group with no experience was small and consequently was totally assigned to the experimental group.

The students involved were predominantly graduate students in a school of social work. The age range was 21 to 35 with a median of 24; 80% were female, 88% had no children of their own, and 80% had previous contact with a mentally retarded individual usually through work experience.

References

Begab, M. J. Impact of education on social work students' knowledge and attitudes about mental retardation. *American Journal of Mental Deficiency*, 1970, 74(6), 801-808.

Hersh, A. & Brown, G. Preparation of mental health personnel for the delivery of mental retardation services. *Community Mental Health Journal*, in preparation.

Krishef, C. & Levine, D.L. Preparing the social worker for effective services to the retarded. *Mental Retardation*, 1968, 6(3), 307.

Prothero, J. C. & Ehlers, W. H. Social work students' attitudes and knowledge changes following study of programmed materials. *American Journal of Mental Deficiency*, 1974, 79(1), 83-86.

Certification Programs in Trainable Mentally Handicapped

WILLIAM H. BERDINE
DOROTHY KELLY

A competency based teacher education (CBTE) program has been developed that approximates the clinical teaching model of Schwartz and Oseroff (1975) in conjunction with the Decision Model for Diagnostic Teaching (Cartwright, Cartwright, & Ysseldyke, 1973). The program is designed to train competencies required for teacher certification in the trainable mentally handicapped area. It was developed to meet a change in state teacher certification for special educators and as one program within the development of a cross categorical special education teacher certification program (i.e., a mild learning and behavior disabilities, severely multiply handicapped, early childhood special education, and special education/vocational program).

The training sequence for the certification program was developed over a 2 year systematic process period following the model proposed by Blackhurst (1974) for CBTE program development, as shown in Figure 1.

Program Components

The trainable mentally handicapped teacher certification program consists of the following seven general teacher functions: educational assessment, characteristics of moderate developmental retardation, educational programing, curriculum design model programs, instructional materials, field experience, and student internship. The seven function areas are subdivided into 17 training competencies. These deal with specific aspects of the general teacher functions (e.g., effective parent conferencing, classroom observation and data systems, use of direct observation instrumentation, medical consideration of the moderately developmentally retarded).

Competency Training Modules

The training competencies are functionally broken down into performance based, individualized training modules. The training modules are designed into autoinstructional and tutorial formats of instruction (depending upon the task required). These formats are anticipated to best facilitate students in demonstrating competence across task areas relating to the general function area in question and specifically for each function's stated competencies.

Entry into the Program

The student enters the trainable mentally handicapped program after successful completion of a survey course titled "An Introduction to Exceptional Children." Upon entry into the program, the student is expected to progress through the competency areas prior to program recommendation for teacher certification. All modules of instruction that are informative in nature or content have pretests available for students to demonstrate mastery of the competency area. The

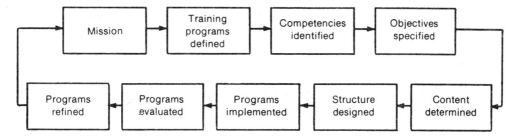

use of pretests in these modules facilitates student movement toward in situ or classroom oriented modules. The modules and competency areas where teaching and classroom management are being taught have no provision for pretesting but rather require performance of the skill areas by the faculty supervisors.

Assessment of Mastery

The assessment of criterion performance or mastery of the training competencies is achieved through two procedures: All content or information modules have pretests and posttests to assess acquisition; the performance or experiential competency modules require observational data collection instrumentation. The Teacher Intern Performance Rating Scale (Berdine, Cegelka, & Kelly, 1977) has been developed to assess the performance of students in experiential settings.

Conclusion

The model for a trainable mentally handicapped teacher training program in a competency based instructional design described above represents one aspect of a larger special education teacher training endeavor. One of the problems identified during the development of the model was that of creating a training endeavor that tended to isolate its trainees and staff from other training programs. The emphasis on demonstrating mastery of competency areas tends toward a tunnel vision perspective for the participants.

Specific efforts need to be taken to demonstrate to the trainee in such CBTE programs how and when they fit into the total services delivery system of education for exceptional children.

The program discussed here is in the program implemented phase of the model. The last two phases of developmental process, programs evaluation and programs refinement, are scheduled to begin upon completion of the 1976-1977 academic year. A 1 year operation period is anticipated as being necessary to make data based program design changes. Modules of instruction and assessment of mastery instrumentation are anticipated to be ready for dissemination at that time.

References

Berdine, W. H., Cegelka, P. T., & Kelly, D. *Teacher intern performance rating scale.* Article submitted for publication, 1977.

Blackhurst, A. E. Some practical considerations in implementing competency-based special education programs. In J. H. Creamer & J. T. Gilmore, *Design for competency based education in special education.* Conference report presented at Syracuse University, 1974.

Cartwright, G. P., Cartwright, C. A., & Ysseldyke, F. S. Two decision models: Identification and diagnostic teaching of handicapped children in the regular classroom. *Psychology in the Schools,* 1973, *10,* 4-11.

Schwartz, L., & Oseroff, A. *The clinical teacher for special education—Final report (Vol. 1).* Washington DC: US Department of Health, Education, and Welfare, 1975.

New Laws for the Handicapped Are Creating New Maturity in Our Schools

Eleanor Roth

In a White House ceremony on March 2, Mrs. Rosalynn Carter accepted the final report of the White House Conference on Handicapped Individuals on behalf of the president. After accepting the report, the First Lady said, "In the past, we as a nation have shied away from anybody who was a little bit different, and yet one of the great strengths of our country has always been the broad diversity of our people. It's time for all of us to recognize that the lack of sight, the absence of hearing, the loss of a limb, or the label of being a former mental patient can no longer be used as an excuse to isolate or discriminate against thirty-six million people who are handicapped."

Until this year the thirty-two mentally retarded youngsters now attending the New Bedford High School's greater school structure attended class in one schoolroom in an elementary school. But when the Education for All Handicapped Children Act (Federal Law P.O. 94-142, similar to the Massachusetts Chapter 766 Statute) went into effect, in the autumn of 1977, sweeping changes were demanded, for this law stated that no handicapped child could be required to attend a school in which the age range of the other students was more than three years above or below his age level.

The intention of the law was to provide a greater degree of interchange between the general student body and the special-needs students, yet it would be necessary to instruct these special students in a self-contained section of the school. How, the administrators wondered, could these young people, ranging in age between sixteen and twenty-two, whose older bodies held immature minds, be absorbed into their new environment in a meaningful manner?

Some of these people are microcephalic; some are macrocephalic. Others are victims of Down's syndrome (they are more commonly known as mongoloids). Technically, they are classified as "moderately learning-disabled." Their I.Q.'s range from approximately twenty to fifty.

The first day I visited this program, I watched Gary Crowell, tri-captain of the football team, helping a boy

While Theodore Calnan, headmaster of the school, pondered the problem, Judith Bolton, a guidance counselor, approached him with a plan. Perhaps they could approach student leaders for help. And why not the football team? These boys might be willing to venture into questionable territory, because, as she phrased it, "football players have already proved themselves."

With Mr. Calnan's nod of approval, Mrs. Bolton spoke to the football squad. Two of the three tri-captains volunteered their help along with other players. And volunteers came from other areas. Some were not student leaders, but student "doubtfuls," even very doubtfuls. But they wanted to help; and so far, not one of the forty-plus volunteers has left the program.

When these retarded youngsters entered the high school last fall there was a general apprehension that they might be ridiculed. "But it never happened!" Richard Bolton, Mrs. Bolton's older son, told me. "Yes, these kids' behavior is childish. They're apt to hug and kiss a student-volunteer in the hall like a three-year-old, without having any sense of its being inappropriate. But the volunteers took it in stride. It was worth it to them to see the tremendous pride these kids felt in their 'friends.'"

Before the new law went into effect, these youngsters had only about two-and-a-half hours of schooling each

"New Laws for the Handicapped are Creating New Maturity in Our Schools," E. Roth, *The Humanist*, January/February 1979. ©1979 by *The Humanist*, a publication of the American Humanist Association.

day. Now they arrive at 7:50 A.M. and leave at 2:15 P.M. count the number of circles on a mimeographed sheet of paper. (There were ten.)

"Do you know what surprises me?" I asked, as Gary looked up at me. "I'm so happy to see that these youngsters' expressions aren't as vacant as I'd expected them to be."

Gary smiled at me. "No," he answered. "They don't look vacant because they're happy."

That evening I spoke with Dr. Alan Leitman, an educator who has been involved with various forms of learning problems. I told him how surprised I was to see people with such minimal I.Q.'s functioning as well as the ones I had observed.

"Intelligence, when measured by any written instrument, represents the degree of environmental deprivation, and deprivation in this type of kid has been compounded," he told me. "They've been deprived of stimulation. People give retarded kids less opportunity to see the world directly, and their environment is terribly constrained."

I knew how delighted they were when they were given an opportunity to meet someone. Earlier that day I'd shaken hands with each student in the program, as we exchanged names.

"I'm Mrs. Roth," I told them.

"Mrs. Roth-Honey?"

"Just Mrs. Roth, not Mrs. Roth-Honey!" Mrs. Elena Lovett, their teacher, said firmly. Then, smiling, she shook her head. "We call them 'honey' very naturally, but we must remind ourselves not to. They imitate everything we do, so they add 'honey' after everyone's name."

"Why bother to correct them?" I asked. "It's sort of sweet."

"No," Mrs. Lovett insisted. "It's inappropriate. We can't encourage behavior that will be inappropriate when they leave us."

This year's special-needs program got under way so rapidly that Mrs. Bolton and the other teachers could only provide the student volunteers with an abbreviated orientation, but plans are being made to provide more extensive preparation for them next year. The students aren't alone in volunteering their time. Some of the teachers, including a gym teacher and an arts teacher, offered their help, which enabled the youngsters to enjoy gym and pottery sessions.

A good deal of attention is given to cleanliness and personal grooming in the life-experience classroom. Besides learning to make a bed, operate a vacuum, and set a table, the youngsters take showers. Supervision is required for this. Girl volunteers teach the girls how to wash and style their hair, and the boys are taught to use electric razors.

Dr. Leitman was pleased to hear this. "That really is excellent," he told me. "That is exactly the kind of touching and affectionate attention these kids desperately need."

Mrs. Judith Underwood, a physical therapist, visits these children periodically. Some of them have physical,

Student volunteer Paul Siva (left) received a Rotary Club Award for his work with the retarded in the New Bedford High School and other local institutions.

as well as mental, handicaps. "These children's poor coordination is not entirely the result of disabilities," she told me. "Often, these kids are not played with as small children. They aren't tossed around like normal babies because they're thought to be too fragile, so they never have the opportunity to develop their motor skills." She used a balloon to play a tossing game with the children. The balloon moves more slowly than a ball and helps the youngsters to develop hand-eye coordination.

These special classes are departmentalized, so the youngsters are exposed to a variety of teachers, teaching aides, and student volunteers. Academics, taught by Mrs. Julie Sequin, are geared to the skills that will be needed for job placement, such as telling time and doing simple arithmetic. A third classroom serves as a center where simple carpentry and pre-vocational skills are taught. Some students are being trained for placement in a supervised employee position. Hopefully, others will work in sheltered workshops after they leave the school.

As the youngsters gathered for lunch, I commented on their orderliness. "They're very good at routine," Mrs. Lovett told me. "They know what they're supposed to do."

The youngsters received no curious attention from the general students as they walked down the corridors, and this not only aids their increasing self-confidence, it also has benefits for the nonhandicapped students. The exposure to "differences" that these "normal" students are receiving will help them to be more sensitive adults. Since increasing numbers of handicapped people are leaving institutions to enter community life, an unselfconscious acceptance by our general population will greatly ease their transition.

Although these youngsters eat at a particular group of tables, teachers, teaching aides, and student volunteers are liberally sprinkled among them. They manage their utensils with a fair degree of deftness, and I wondered whether the student volunteers were purposely maintaining their own manners more carefully than students at the other tables, since they knew how precisely they would be imitated.

Some things have gone more smoothly than had been anticipated, but there are problems. These youngsters must be accompanied to the bathrooms. They need only be accompanied—they do not require help with their personal needs—and the student volunteers have been enormously helpful in simply providing enough people for this purpose. And, though these retarded youngsters usually seem cheerful and happy, working with them involves more than receiving joyful smiles.

The frustrations that these people feel because of their inability to express themselves can lead to emotional disturbances. Since the least-retarded people also have the greatest degree of awareness, they often feel a greater sense of their own inadequacy. And, like everyone else, these kids have moods and can become angry, but they don't know how to cope with their feelings.

Since a large segment of the population in New Bedford is Portuguese, some of the retarded youngsters speak only that language. A number of the student volunteers and teachers speak Portuguese fluently, but the youngsters are encouraged to speak in English. It will be necessary for them to speak English when they leave the school.

Manny Pinhancos, a student volunteer, has excellent rapport with these youngsters. When he enters a room their faces shine. "Manny!" they exclaim. "Manny-Honey is here!"

As Manny entered the classroom the day of my visit, Louis, one of the retarded youngsters, remained silent. The single exception in the class. He did not even lift his face to acknowledge Manny's presence.

"What's the matter with Louis?" Manny asked the teacher.

"He's been withdrawn all day," the instructor answered. "We haven't been able to get him to respond at all."

"You're not even going to say 'hello' to me?" Manny asked Louis.

Louis apparently couldn't bear to hurt someone he admired and had grown to love. Leaving his chair, he walked forward from the back of the room and extended his hand to Manny.

"Manny my friend?" His voice rose questioningly.

"Of course I'm your friend, Louis!" Manny assured him.

Louis's sudden smile lit the room. "Manny *my* friend!" His voice held pride.

Manny has a particularly good rapport with Valerie, a retarded child who is also deaf and mute. He is learning sign language so he can communicate with her, and her eyes dance as his fingers move swiftly with a special message for her. Eagerly, she forms her own signs in response. Though she can neither speak nor hear, she feels loved and accepted, and she laughs with the purest delight.

Mark Touhey, another student volunteer, is a tall, good-looking member of the swimming team.

"Do many of your friends come?" I asked him.

"Some kids like it, some don't. But, you know, you come for a while. You might back off at first, but the kids kind of grow on you. They react to you. You get your own little jokes with them. You stop thinking of them as retarded and think of them as just being 'younger' kids."

I noticed one of the girls looking at him wistfully, and I asked "Is it ever awkward with the girls?"

"Some of the girls get crushes on you . . . They give you little presents . . . but you gotta be sensitive about it. It's very real to them."

"Do you think that your participation in the program encourages others to volunteer?"

"Well," he spoke disparagingly, "everyone knows the jocks. I guess they figure that if we can do it, it can't be that bad. I don't feel that I'm doing very much, but it represents a lot to the kids. They try to be buddy-buddy with us. They talk about it and they talk about themselves." He grinned. "Bob talks about his 'girl friend.' Mike asks me where my car is. The thing is, they brighten up and feel alive and are interested!"

Gary Crowell (right), a flexible individual who moves swiftly on the football field, enjoys being patient with others.

"The school administrators were really expecting these kids to be harassed."

"You mean by little freshmen? By kids who can't take care of themselves? No. That hasn't happened. The main thing is that if these kids feel accepted in the school they'll have more control and experience being around people. It will be much easier for them outside." He paused, then added thoughtfully, "Up to now, almost everything has been done for them. Sure, they'll always live a simple life, but at least they'll be more self-sufficient."

Gary Crowell, the football, hockey, and track star I'd spoken to earlier, told me how he and his fellow football players had responded when Coach Bruce MacPherson described the program to them.

"Some of them didn't think they could hack it, and the coach didn't pressure them to come."

"You've been a real leader in terms of these kids being accepted," I told him.

Gary shrugged. "I'm glad if I have, but some of the other high school kids still can't accept them. The way I figure it, if some high school kids are so immature that they can't accept these kids, then we have to accept *that*, too—that people just react differently."

"Has your experience working with these kids affected you in any way?"

"Yes. I'm thinking of becoming a gym teacher for students requiring special education."

We turned to look out of the window then. It was snowing heavily outside and Wayne, a victim of Down's syndrome, shook his head fearfully. "I hate snow," he muttered.

"Wayne hates snow because he can't walk very well in it," Gary murmured. "You know, some of these kids' appearances can deceive you. They don't seem as different as they are. Take David, for instance. He can learn something fairly quickly, but he'll forget it—almost right away. Some kids simply can't retain knowledge. Some-

times we teach them the same thing over and over again, one day after the other . . . It takes a lot of patience; but still, they're better off here than where they were before."

Several weeks after observing this program I went to Washington, D.C., where I spoke to Mrs. Patricia Forsythe, staff director for Senator Randolph's subcommittee on the handicapped. Since that office had received very little feed-back from schools across the country in terms of their implementation of this law, she was extremely pleased to hear about New Bedford's experience with student volunteers. She even suggested that I write to the director of the Office of Handicapped Individuals in the Hubert H. Humphrey Building to let him know about the New Bedford experiment.

As I jotted the address down I made a mental note to write to Senator Muriel Humphrey, too. I knew the senator had a retarded grandchild and that she had long been involved with problems regarding the handicapped.

I wrote to her as soon as I got home. After describing the program, I expressed my personal feelings: "Certainly, when we treat our normal youngsters with respect, when we permit them to participate in helping to solve society's problems, we help them to mature . . . Given responsibilities, our youngsters surprise us with their resourcefulness and their competence. Presented with a challenge, they more than rise to meet it."

Despite her demanding schedule, Senator Humphrey responded with surprising promptness. "I found your observations interesting," she replied, "and was encouraged by the conclusion that the efforts of schools to adapt to the needs of handicapped children develop greater social maturity among regular students."

It seems apparent to many educators that these new laws can benefit more than just the various learning-handicapped children. They can help the entire school population to come of age.

Instruction and Training of the Trainable Mentally Handicapped

Moderately mentally handicapped individuals can learn and perform in appropriate educational programs. Too often these individuals were left to vegetate or perform only repetitive, menial tasks which did little to improve skills or approach potential.

A very important aspect of the education of the trainable mentally handicapped is an affective one. Support, praise, and love can greatly improve self-image and positive attitude on the part of the trainable mentally handicapped student. Success breeds success, and a healthy attitude exhibited by the teacher can initially foster this success, and then effectively reinforce continuing success.

Recognition of personal self worth is one of the aspects of today's education for the handicapped.

In order to ensure appropriate programs for the trainable retarded, more competent teachers and administrators of programs for the handicapped must be developed. Just as important is parental cooperation and involvement. Without the support of parents our school programs will not reach *their* full potential and will find it difficult in helping the trainable mentally handicapped reach *their* full potential.

A Counseling Program for TMR Students

Margie I. Norman

Margie I. Norman is Special Education
Counselor, Austin Elementary Opportunity
School, San Antonio Independent School
District, Texas.

In *Educating Exceptional Children*, Kirk describes the trainable mentally retarded (TMR) child as

One who, because of sub-normal intelligence, is not capable of learning in classes for the educable mentally retarded but who does have potentialities for learning (1) self-care, (2) adjustment to the home or neighborhood, and (3) economic usefulness in the home, a sheltered workshop, or an institution. (1972, p. 164)

The U.S. Department of Health, Education and Welfare's Committee on Mental Retardation states that moderately retarded youngsters can learn to talk or to communicate; have poor social awareness; fair motor development; profit from training in self-help; and can be managed with moderate supervision. Such children can usually achieve social and vocational skills adequate to minimum self-support but may need guidance and assistance when under unusual social or economic stress. They can profit from training in social and occupational skills but are unlikely to progress beyond second-grade level in academic subjects. Severely retarded children are more handicapped: They have poor motor development; speech is minimal; they have little or no communication skills; but some can profit from systematic habit training.

The students at Austin Opportunity School in the San Antonio, Tex., Independent School District have been classified as TMR. This category encompasses a range of intellectual functioning from moderately to severely retarded. In the recent past, this depressed level of functioning automatically excluded these students from guidance programs. Many educators believed that severely retarded youngsters could not profit from counseling.

A study was made to determine the ways that retarded students differed from typical clients. This study enabled me to devise a program to meet the needs of these children. The study found that, contrary to popular belief, some severely retarded children do suffer from emotional problems. One difficulty in working with these students lay in the fact that because of their handicap they had been treated differently and had learned to respond in a particular way. It was my contention that these children could be reprogrammed to new patterns of response. Because of their retardation they would necessarily have to endure much repetition.

In the 1975–76 school year, a group-guidance program was initiated for these students. Groups of eight children met with me each week to listen to stories about children and the problems that they encountered. Discussion followed that permitted the students to relate their own experiences and to discuss ways of handling problems. This kind of activity helped the students develop the capacity to understand their own feelings and reactions to others so that they could have control over their own actions. The children also were helped to develop language and social skills.

There were five groups of eight students each. Students were selected for group work after several conferences with each teacher. Of the eight students in each group, one or two were considered to be more outgoing and verbal and had displayed at least minimal leadership qualities. The other students generally had some problem that the teachers felt needed attention. For example, one student had been diagnosed as autistic, several had limited expressive language skills, some displayed acting-out behavior, and some were withdrawn and uncommunicative.

The problems that I encountered in attempting to launch this venture were numerous. Learning the group process proved to be tedious. Most of these students tended to have poor memories and required many drill-like exercises. At the same time, stories and activities had to be tailored to meet their levels of understanding and interest. Problems were compounded by the fact that the students had the physical development of adults (students' ages ranged 13 to 21) and the mental age of 4- or 5-year-old children. Many of the students were unmotivated and had long ago adopted a "Why try?" attitude. Each step forward was viewed as a major accomplishment.

Some of the students had difficulty adjusting to a change in their normal school routine. One 18-year-old female, Linda, was subject to abrupt mood changes: One minute she would be smiling and cooperative, the next screaming, crying, and rolling on the floor. Phillip, a 21 year old, often displayed an uncontrollable temper. At times he would shout loudly and begin to stutter. His stuttering served to infuriate him further, and he was apt to throw things. Elias, who was 17, frequently became severely withdrawn. At times he would become mesmerized by the movement of his fingers, by a button on his shirt, or any similiar

"A Counseling Program for TMR Students," M. Normal, *The School Counselor*, Vol. 24, No. 4, March 1977. ©1977 by the American Personnel and Guidance Association.

object on which he could focus his attention. He would not respond to his name, to questions, or to any other attention-getting device.

Most group members had short attention spans. Sylvia had particular difficulty in this respect. She often would leave her seat to wander around the room shortly after a session had begun. She could be easily persuaded to return to her seat, but she soon wandered off again. Peer pressure eventually caused her to remain seated for increasingly longer periods of time. Michael, on the other hand, always did exactly what anyone told him to do immediately. If he happened to wander into a classmate's territory and the classmate said, "Get out of here, Michael! Go away. Go home!" he would immediately get his coat and leave. This behavior caused a problem because Michael lived 7 or 8 miles away and had no idea where home was.

Initially, we had to engage in extended periods of verbalizing and modeling. Even the verbal students had difficulty responding to questions, thinking of similiar situations in their lives, and in expressing feelings. I learned that many of the youngsters had never had real conversations with adults. Most were accustomed to being told what to do and think. The students tended to respond in one word and to repeat responses as well as behaviors. In many youngsters I observed a rigid sort of behavior and a resistance to change routine. At 15, David was intellectually superior to many in his group. Yet he was so rigid in his behavior that the slightest change in his routine resulted in near trauma. It took quite a long time for him to adjust to coming to group sessions one afternoon a week. For weeks he would sit rigidly and apart from the group, avoiding eye contact, stealing glances at pictures, but not participating in discussion. He was always included in the conversation and invited to join in the activities. Finally, after a long time, we had a breakthrough. I was delighted because I remembered seeing David in the cafeteria one day when another student had inadvertently been seated in "his place." David was so upset by this change in his routine that he could not eat his lunch that day.

Eventually, the groups became accustomed to the change in routine and learned the rudiments of group process. After this the students began to look forward to coming to see the counselor. For example, Tony started checking with me the first day of the week to be sure that he could come

on Thursday for his meeting. He would ask, "Is today the day, teacher?" Alice got in the habit of dropping by my office every morning before she went to her classroom to receive her "warm fuzzy"—a big hug. Although her speech was limited and distorted, she learned to communicate her need for special recognition.

In January of the school year parent groups were started. These groups evolved slowly. Parents were contacted through the PTA and were invited to meet twice a month. It was felt that such meetings might serve to acquaint the parents with the guidance program and might reinforce the training being received by the students. At these meetings discussion centered on the problems and concerns of parents in dealing with retarded youngsters.

Many of the children lived in single-parent homes. The mothers related that their husbands had seemed unable to cope with the fact of a severely retarded child. Some of the adults who came to the meetings were in fact the grandparents of the children. One man who attended had assumed the responsibility of rearing his younger brother after the death of their parents.

The parent group that eventually evolved had to overcome obstacles to get to the meetings. Since the students resided in all sections of a very large school district and were bussed in, there seemed to be no way for the parents to form car pools to come to the school. Several of the mothers rode the school buses with the children and went home on city buses, which necessitated their transferring several times. Two of the mothers had to take time off from their jobs to attend the meetings. One mother brought her baby with her because she could not afford a baby-sitter. Only one mother in the group had a car, and she had to care for her elderly mother who accompanied her.

The discussions purposely were kept low-key so they would be less threatening to the participants. Discussion centered on problems related to the students and the school. There had been incidents of fighting, some students had knives, and there was general disorder on several of the 17 buses that transported the students. These conditions posed definite safety hazards. The safety problem was complicated by the fact that the same buses also took other younger TMR students to another district school. The parents formed a group of volunteers to ride the most troublesome buses to maintain discipline. They also trained reliable students to act as bus monitors

to report any incidents of trouble so that disciplinary action might be taken.

Discussion centered for a time on the services available to the students. Although some students had attended the school for as long as 6 or 8 years, the parents were unaware of what their children had been doing. The parents were not familiar with the curriculum being offered by the school. They did not know of the counseling service, of the compulsory reevaluation of all students, of the psychological or medical service available, or of the sheltered workshop placement service available to all qualified students. After discussion, the information was compiled and printed for parents who were unable to attend the meetings. Printing and distributing this information also served as a drawing card, because more parents made arrangements to attend the meetings.

There were inquiries about summer recreation facilities for TMRs. These inquiries led to some research and produced good results. Several facilities were uncovered. One local church sponsored a nondenominational summer camp on the seacoast. Three of our students received scholarships to attend it. The information about recreational facilities was also printed and distributed.

The last two meetings of the year focused on dealing with students' sexual feelings. This proved to be a very popular subject and one of grave concern to the parents. All of the students were physically mature and had the same sexual feelings and impulses as other adults, but they were emotionally and mentally children.

I felt that a more influential speaker was needed for this important topic, so the school district psychologist was invited to join us. The meeting was begun by having each person introduce himself or herself and explain his or her particular concern. The psychologist then introduced herself and spoke briefly on her background and philosophy. She then turned the discussion back to the parents. The parents' response was overwhelming: It seemed that they had kept unexpressed very strong feelings and concerns about the subject. The parents were most eager to tell of their experiences and to learn from the psychologist whether they had "done right."

The psychologist listened and then gave her recommendations for dealing with the problem. One mother expressed relief that she was on the right track. Two of the mothers were against the psychologist's suggestions for moral or religious reasons. None of the parents seemed shocked or angry. When the meeting time was ended, the parents eagerly asked if they might continue the discussion at the next meeting. They were undismayed by the fact that the psychologist could not be present. They told me, "You know as much as she does. It was nice to have her here, but we don't really need her that much."

At the next meeting, our last of the year, we reviewed the previous discussion and then continued with it. I noted happily that the group was the largest that ever had attended. The discussion was heated and inspiring. Gone was the low-key atmosphere of the first few meetings. Everyone was speaking out, expressing feelings, and discussing a taboo subject with enthusiasm and confidence. The group parted with plans to begin meetings much earlier in the coming school year.

We launched this guidance program for TMR students with minimal guidelines available and with a great deal of trial and error. It was a two-part effort in that I involved the students in one phase and their parents in the other. Although we made mistakes, we felt that we also made gains. We proved to everyone's satisfaction that severely retarded students can learn the rudiments of group process. They can be trained to think through simple problems and articulate solutions. These children learned to interact in new ways, to share feelings, and to be aware of another person's concern.

The parents learned also. They shared more in their children's world away from home. They involved the children in new activities because of things brought out in discussion. They shared ideas, fears, and experiences with each other and learned that they were not alone with their burden.

References

Kirk, S. *Educating exceptional children.* Boston: Houghton Mifflin, 1972.

U.S. Department of Health, Education and Welfare, Secretary's Committee on Mental Retardation. *The problem of mental retardation.* Washington D.C.: 1969.

A VOCATION PROGRAM FOR THE TRAINABLE MENTALLY RETARDED STUDENT

JOSEPH L. SCELFO
Director of Special Needs
Ocean County Vocational-Technical School

JAMES MICALI
Vocational Evaluator

A vocational experience is being provided for trainable mentally retarded students during their secondary school years to prepare them to be contributing workers. This article describes the three phases of a vocational program in operation that is designed to meet the needs of these students in an educationally sequential order.

We have reached the point in time where the trainable mentally retarded student should be involved in a program that is suitable for him within the vocational school environment.

Special Education has come a long way since the early 1960's when it was given much impetus during the Kennedy Administration. Now, however, the classroom curriculum has been developed and refined and a renewed effort to expand and include vocational education as a part of the student's school experience is needed. Self-help skills, recognition words, number concepts and the like are usually reiterated throughout the elementary school and are also a part of the secondary curriculum. While it is true that they must be repeated and reinforced, they do become redundant.

The trainable student will usually terminate his education when state law mandates it because of his age. It is at that time he must go out into the "world of work," be it a sheltered work shop or private industry depending upon his capabilities. However, the transition from the classroom directly to a working situation is often abrupt. A vocational school program designed for the student could be used as the vehicle of transition (as well as a training experience) from the school environment to a work environment.

Indeed, there are programs currently offered for the trainable mentally retarded student in vocational schools, but they are too few and far between. How do these programs work and what are their objectives?

A general description of a program currently in operation is presented here as a guide to demonstrate the procedures and operations. This program could be used either on a part-time or shared time basis.

Purpose

The purpose of a Trainable Program is to provide an environment in which the trainable mentally retarded student can be evaluated and trained for employment in a sheltered workshop or private industry. General objectives of such a program would be: to determine through evaluation the student's potential for occupational training; develop those characteristics recognized as essential for employment, i.e. punctuality, attendance, following directions, completion of assigned tasks, etc.; strengthen the student's ability to get along with co-workers; and to place the student in employment situations.

"A Vocation Program for the Trainable Mentally Retarded Student," J. Scelfo, J. Micali, Education, Vol. 98, No. 4, Summer 1978. © Copyright 1978 by Project Innovation.

2. INSTRUCTION

First Phase: Evaluation

Upon entering the program the student is evaluated through a series of tests to determine the extent of his motor and perceptual skills. Also assessed at this time are behavior, reaction to the tests and to those with whom he must come in contact.

When the evaluation is completed, a profile can be made of the student. Areas of assessment are generally (a) attention span, (b) retention (c) perservation, (d) discrimination among and between items, (e) eye and hand motor coordination, and (f) following directions. Awareness of a problem in any of these areas and how it manifests itself in a working environment is the primary purpose of the evaluation. From this point, the program seeks to develop the skills which are tested to such a degree that the student can use them productively in a working situation within or outside of a sheltered environment.

Second Phase: Simulated Work Activities

The student enters the second phase of the program upon completion of the evaluative process. There are two sections in this phase. The first involves the student working in situations by himself. The second involves him in group activities.

It is during the second phase that attention is given to any problem that was identified during the evaluation. At this time, the student is exposed to a variety of hand-tools and equipment that he will encounter in actual working situations. The student works with these items, learns their names and uses them to the extent that his ability enables him.

It is through a structured approach that the student is taught basic work skills. He follows an organized method of instruction with all work he encounters. Working by himself and using this approach, the student is gradually moved into group activities.

These work activities are recorded and by using a rating scale, his progress can be plotted. On the basis of his progress the student can then enter the third phase.

Third Phase: Work Training Activities

It is during this phase that the student is placed into actual work situations. He may work individually, in a group, or on an assembly line depending on the job he is assigned.

The work the student produces would be designed to have a marketable value. Broad areas could include: plastics, wooden toys, book binding, silk screening and decorative items. The student is exposed to new tools, again through a structured approach, and his skill in using them is continually evaluated. Cooperation with co-workers is emphasized during this time and socially acceptable behavior is also stressed.

A bi-monthly evaluation and written narrative of the student should be made during this phase. He continues working in this phase until he graduates at which time plans are made for him to begin work in a sheltered workshop or, where possible, in private industry.

Conclusion

The Trainable Program as outlined here or any variations of it that are used in vocational schools, offers the student the experience of a real working environment. This experience will allow him to function with varying degrees of success in his future "world of work." The exposure to working with machines and equipment will provide the student with basic skills and work attitudes which will enable him to be productive.

Finally, and most important, is that this vocational program provides the trainable mentally retarded student with the transition from school into an actual working situation within the community.

TEACHING RETARDED PRESCHOOLERS TO IMITATE THE FREE-PLAY BEHAVIOR OF NONRETARDED CLASS-MATES: TRAINED AND GENERALIZED EFFECTS

Charles A. Peck, M.A.
Human Services Associates

Tony Apolloni, Ph.D.
Thomas P. Cooke, Ph.D.
Sonoma State College

Sharon A. Raver, Ed.S.
Santa Rosa Junior College

Two peer-imitation training procedures were applied to increase the imitation between retarded and nonretarded children in integrated preschool settings. Baseline observations revealed low rates of imitation and social interaction between retarded and nonretarded classmates under naturalistic conditions. A simple training procedure, consisting of adult-delivered prompts and social reinforcement, was employed to increase the retarded children's imitation of their nonretarded classmates' free-play behavior. Demonstrations of training effects were made utilizing both multi-element baseline and multiple baseline designs. Data collected under nontraining conditions indicated maintenance of peer-imitation effects. Increases in reciprocal social interaction between retarded and nonretarded children were also noted under taining and nontraining conditions.

Many "integrated" preschool programs have been recently established to provide educational programming for mixed groups of retarded and nonretarded children (Apolloni & Cooke, 1977; Wynne, Ulfelder, & Dakof, 1975). Retarded children are expected to profit from exposure to developmentally typical peer-models and from numerous opportunities to learn adaptive ways to socially interact with nonretarded peers (Bricker & Bricker, 1972). Still, direct observation research on the efficacy of integrated programming (Guralnick, 1976; Snyder, Apolloni, & Cooke, 1977; Wynne, Ulfelder, & Dakof, 1975) has not substantiated that positive outcomes *necessarily* result from such arrangements. Observers of integrated preschool settings have consistently noted minimal levels of peer imitation and interaction between handicapped and nonhandicapped classmates (Allen, Benning, & Drummond, 1972). It seems that special teaching procedures are required if educationally desirable out-comes are to reliably emanate from integrated preschools.

Recent research has demonstrated that increases in handicapped children's imitation of peers can be achieved under structured training conditions (Apolloni, Cooke, & Cooke, 1977; Cooke, Cooke, & Apolloni, in press; Guralnick, 1976). None of these studies, however, has demonstrated increases in generalized imitation under unstructured conditions.

The present study assessed the effects of direct peer-imitation training between retarded and nonretarded children in naturalistic, free-play situations. Two experiments are reported. In Experiment 1, dyadic social interaction data (Strain, Cooke, & Apolloni, 1976) were collected under training and nontraining conditions regarding the extent to which: (a) retarded children imitated and socially interacted with nonretarded peers, and (b) nonretarded children imitated and socially interacted with retarded peers. Additionally, in Experiment 2, dyadic data were collected on the affective nature (positive or negative) of social interaction between retarded children and a nonretarded peer-model. The purpose of both experiments was to assess the generality of social behavior changes achieved through peer-imitation training under free-field conditions.

EXPERIMENT 1: METHOD

Subjects and settings

The investigation was conducted in an experimental preschool in Santa Rosa, Calif. The classroom served six mentally retarded children between 3 and 5 years old. Three nonretarded children (peer-models) from a nearby nursery school were present in the classroom for daily, 30-minute, free-play periods.

The study was conducted 5 days weekly, Monday through Friday, in a class-room that measured 8 m × 13 m. Training and generalization sessions were conducted in a 4 m × 4 m free-play area partitioned from the rest of the classroom. The same materials were present in the free-play area each day: a rectangular table, several chairs, two simple puzzles, a set of small building blocks, two toy telephones, a toy stove, a toy sink with dishes, dress-up clothes, a teeter totter, a piano, and several picture books. The individuals in the free-play situation included either one or two adults, five retarded children, and three peer-models.

The retarded subjects were three children, two males and one female, each of whom had been medically diagnosed as having Down's syndrome. A standardized assessment was made of each subject using the Vineland Social Maturity Scale (VSMS) and the Denver Developmental Screening Test (DDST). The results of these tests indicated that each subject was functioning at a moderately developmentally delayed level. Subject 1 (male) was 38 months of age at the time of the experiment; he scored an age equivalent of 1.97 on the VSMS. Subject 2 (female) was 36 months of age, and scored 1.65 on the VSMS. Subject 3 (male) was 37 months old; he scored 1.8 on the VSMS. All three subjects were rated delayed on the DDST.

The three peer-models were normally functioning children who exhibited typical developmental patterns. Peer-models 1 (male), 2 (female), and 3 (male) were 59, 50, and 49 months of age, respectively, at the beginning of the study.

Procedure

Observations and training procedures were the same for all three subjects.

Observation system. Data were collected by one or two observers during all training and generalization sessions. A time-sampling technique was employed to record the imitation and social interaction of both the retarded subjects and peer-models during training and generalization sessions. The response events monitored for the retarded subjects and the peer-models were as follows:

A. Peer-imitation: A response similar in topography to one emitted 5 seconds or less previously by another child and which was observed by the second child.

B. Social interaction: The class of performance, which includes one or more of the following response events:

Vocalizing — All vocal utterances emitted while the child is directly facing another child or vocalizations emitted while not facing another child but which, by virtue of content (e.g., proper name, "hey you," etc.) and/or accompanying motor gestural movements (e.g., waving, pointing), clearly indicate that a child is directing the utterance to another child.

Social gesturing — All motor responses which involve waving, extending arms, or gesturing directly towards another child, or motor responses which cause a child's hand(s) or an object held in a child's hand(s) to come into direct contact with the body of another child. Accidental physical contacts, i.e., ones in which there is no follow-up response by the subject who made the contact with his hand(s) or no response by the child who was the recipient of the contact (other than that made by an inanimate object given the same treatment), were not considered social gestures.

Sharing — A child offering, giving, or receiving an object or material to or from another child, or his concurrent use of an object or material with another child. Both children must simultaneously touch the material with at least one hand, unless the material is designed to be used visually, consists of many small objects comprising a set, or is shoved, rolled, or thrown from one child to another and caught with the hands.

Vocalizing, social gesturing, and/or sharing response events emitted one second or longer following the subject's most recent social interaction response were coded as separate instances.

For purposes of assessing interobserver agreement, training and generalization sessions were divided into 10-second intervals indicated by recorded signals. The responses of each retarded subject, the training events (adult instructions, physical prompts, and/or praise), and the responses of the peer-models in interaction with the retarded subject being observed were recorded by the observers on prepared coding sheets.

The dyadic nature of the coding system enabled the observers to record the imitation and social interaction of both the target subject and any other child (retarded or peer-model) with whom he might interact.

Interobserver agreement. Two observers simultaneously collected data during training and generalization sessions for all subjects at least three times per experimental condition. Levels of interobserver agreement were calculated on each of the responses for each subject. This was done by dividing the number of observer agreements by the number of observer agreements plus disagreements.

Experimental design

The effects of the training procedure were assessed using a combined multiple baseline across subjects and a multi-element baseline design (Ulman & Sulzer-Azaroff, 1975). The experimental conditions were as follows:

Pretraining. The individuals present in the Pretraining setting were: three retarded subjects, three peer-models, two retarded peers who were not subjects, and one female adult. The session lasted 30 minutes. Observation was focused on one retarded subject at a time. The adult did not initiate interaction with the children and terminated contact as quickly as possible when subjects initiated interaction with her. No training procedure was in effect to modify any of the targeted behaviors of the retarded subjects or their nonretarded peers.

Training Period I. This condition resembled Pretraining except that a teacher entered the free-play area and intervened for 4 minutes to increase Subject 1's levels of imitative behavior. Instructions were delivered when subjects were within proximity (3 ft or less) of a peer-model engaged in appropriate material use. When necessary, the teacher physically prompted proximity. The following instructions were issued: "Look! See what he/she is doing?" (Teacher points to peer-model.) "You do it." If the subject imitated the behavior of the peer-model within 5 seconds, he/she was socially praised with the verbal compliment of "Good boy/girl, you did what he/she did!" and positive physical contact consisting of a pat or hug. If the retarded subject did not imitate the peer-model, he/she was physically prompted through the behavior and then praised. No procedure was implemented in Training Period I to modify the imitation or social interaction of the other two subjects. Subject 1 was prompted to imitate each of the three peer-models at least once per training session.

Training Period II. Conditions described for Training Period I were maintained. Additionally, the training procedure delineated in Training Period I was applied with Subject 2.

Training Period III. Conditions described for Training Period II were maintained. Additionally, the training procedure described for Training Period I was implemented with Subject 3.

Generalization Period. The teacher left the free-play area immediately following each 4-minute training period and remained out of the subjects' sight for 3 minutes. Data were collected to assess the extent to which newly learned peer-imitative behavior would generalize to a setting free of adult-imposed contingencies. Assessment was also made of the effects of the training procedure on the levels of social responding between the retarded subject and the peer-models.

EXPERIMENT 1: RESULTS

Interobserver agreement

Levels of observer agreement were calculated on a cell-by-cell basis by including only cells in which entries were coded. Levels of interobserver agreement for imitative responding across all three subjects ranged from .81 to 1.00, with a mean of .87.

Interobserver agreement for social interaction from subjects to peer-models ranged from .83 to 1.00 with a mean of .95. Agreement on social interaction from peer-models to subjects ranged from .93 to 1.00, with a mean of .96.

Interobserver agreement on training events for all subjects ranged from .80 to 1.00, with a mean of .96 and a mode of 1.00.

Imitation

Data presented in Figure 1 indicate that levels of imitative responding increased for each subject concomitant with the introduction of the training procedure. Physically prompted imitations are not included in these data. Gains were shown under both training and nontraining conditions for all subjects. Subject 1's pretraining rate of imitation of peer-models was zero for each session. Under training conditions, Subject 1's rate of imitation rose immediately and remained at an increased level throughout the study. For Subject 1, increases in generalized imitative behavior under nontraining conditions were observed during 50% of the sessions after training began.

Subject 2 also demonstrated zero levels of imitative behavior during the pretraining period. Immediate increases in imitative behavior were observed for Subject 2 under training conditions. Increases in generalized imitation were also noted for Subject 2.

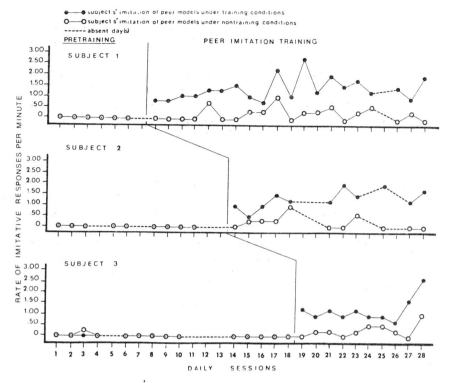

Figure 1. Rate per minute of handicapped children's imitation of nonhandicapped children under training and nontraining conditions.

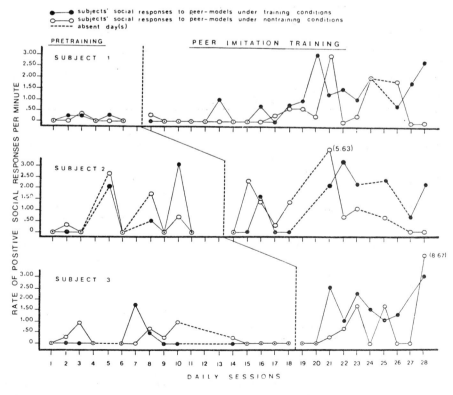

Figure 2. Rate per minute of handicapped children's social responses to nonhandicapped children under training and nontraining conditions.

2. INSTRUCTION

Subject 3 demonstrated near-zero levels of imitative behavior throughout the Pretraining period. Subject 3's rate of imitative behavior increased with the onset of the training. Generalized imitation was observed for Subject 3.

The data collected on the peer-model's rates of imitation of the retarded subjects showed that there was no substantial imitation of the retarded children by peer-models. No instances of peer-model imitation of target subjects were observed under training conditions throughout the study. Three instances of a peer-model imitating a target subject were observed during the 246 minutes of observation under nontraining conditions.

Social interaction

Figure 2 illustrates that rates of social interaction between the retarded subjects and the peer-models increased subsequent to implementation of the imitation training procedure for Subjects 1 and 3. Subject 2's rate of social response toward the peer-models was not clearly affected by the training procedure. Figure 3 shows reciprocal increases in social interaction directed toward Subjects 1 and 3 by the peer-models. The increase in interaction between the peer-models and Subject 1 occurred concomitant with the introduction of peer-imitation training with Subject 3. The peers' rate of social behavior toward Subject 2 was not clearly affected by the imitation training.

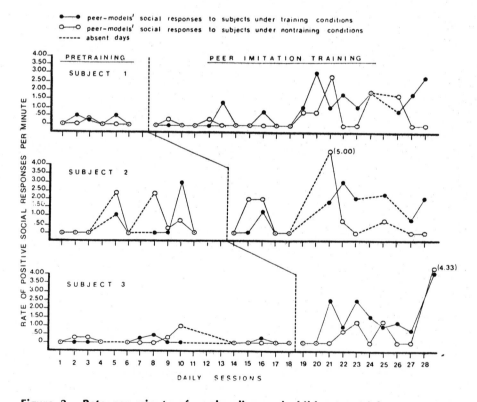

Figure 3. Rate per minute of nonhandicapped children's social responses to handicapped children under training and nontraining conditions.

TABLE 1
RATE PER MINUTE OF TRAINING EVENTS FOR EACH SUBJECT (EXPERIMENT 1)

	Instructions	Physical prompts	Consequations
Subject 1			
Mean	1.33	.06	1.35
Range	.50–3.0	.00–.5	.75–2.25
Subject 2			
Mean	1.23	.02	1.27
Range	.75–1.5	.00–.25	.50–2.0
Subject 3			
Mean	1.85	.30	1.60
Range	1.25–2.25	.00–.75	1.0–2.25

Training events

Table 1 represents a quantification of the behavior of the adult trainer directed to each subject in Experiment 1.

EXPERIMENT 2: METHOD

Subjects and setting

An integrated toddler stimulation project served as the location for Experiment 2. Training and generalization sessions were conducted in a partitioned 1.8 m × 2 m area of a 12.3 m × 9.2 m classroom. The same materials were present in the training area each day: books, modeling clay, balls, donut and spindle sets, wooden pounding benches and hammers, scarves, telephones, necklaces, adult clothes, mirrors, trucks, baby dolls, liquid bubbles, windmills, and xylophones. During training sessions materials were kept in a box and presented one at a time during the appropriate activity. All the toys were left out during pretraining and generalization sessions. Those present in both training and generalization environments each day included one target subject, one peer-model, and one adult trainer.

One normally developing 44-month-old male participated as the peer-model in Experiment 2. One female, 25 months old at the onset of the study, and one male, 34 months old, were the target subjects. Their IQ scores were 46 and 74, respectively. Both subjects demonstrated low rates of parallel and solitary play prior to study. One adult staff member from the infant project served as the trainer during all training sessions.

Procedure

Observation and training procedures were the same for both subjects.

Observational system. One or two observers employed a time-sampling procedure to record the following response events for both the subjects and the peer-model.

A. Positive social interaction: A touch with hand(s), hug, kiss, wave, and/or any cooperative response(s) involved in sharing a toy or material. Positive social interaction was also defined as a vocalization directed to another child, excluding screams, shouts, cries, whines, or other utterances which indicated negative social behavior.

B. Negative social interaction: A hit, pinch, kick, butt with the head, nonplayful push or pull, grabbing objects from another child, destroying the construction of another child, as well as screams, shouts, cries, whines, or other utterances which were accompanied by negative social behavior.

C. Imitation of another child: A response similar in topography to one emitted 5 seconds or less previously by another child and which was observed by the second child.

2. INSTRUCTION

In a fashion similar to Experiment 1, the data were collected on prepared coding sheets. Data were collected during 3-minute training sessions on the subjects' imitative and social behaviors. No data were gathered on the peer-model's behavior during training sessions. Three-minute generalization sessions immediately followed each training session. A dyadic observational system was employed during generalization sessions to permit observers to record the imitation and social interaction of both the subjects and the peer-model.

Interobserver agreement

Levels of interobserver agreement were assessed and calculated in the same manner as for Experiment 1.

Experimental design

A multi-element baseline design (Ulman & Sulzer-Azaroff, 1975) was employed to assess the effects of the training procedure. The following experimental conditions were implemented:

Pretraining.   Three individuals were present in each 6-minute Pretraining session: the target subject, the peer-model, and the adult trainer. During Pretraining sessions, the trainer remained in a corner of the free-play area visually attending to a book. The trainer did not initiate interaction with the target subject or the peer-model and terminated interaction initiated by them as quickly as possible. No training procedure was in effect to modify the behavior of the retarded subjects or the peer-model.

Training.   The procedures were the same for both subjects. Those present for each 3-minute training session included one target subject, one peer-model, and the trainer. A training package was employed, consisting of songs accompanied by motor gestures, direct instructions (e.g., "See what he's doing? You do that."), physical prompts, and praise for approximations and appropriate imitative responses.

The trainer introduced the training toys one at a time and prompted the subject and the peer-model to play simultaneously with each toy. Song lyrics describing play behaviors were initiated to encourage the children to appropriately manipulate the available materials. Target subjects were instructed to imitate the peer-model. If a subject failed to respond immediately, the trainer physically prompted desired behaviors.

Generalization.   Directly following each training session, the target subject and peer-model were observed for 3 minutes. Generalization conditions were the same as those for Pretraining.

EXPERIMENT 2: RESULTS

Interobserver agreement

Levels of interobserver agreement were calculated in the same manner as for Experiment 1. Interobserver agreement on imitation from subjects to peer-models in training and generalization sessions ranged from .82 to 1.00, with a mean of .90. Interobserver agreement on social interaction behaviors on the part of the peer-model and subjects ranged from .70 to 1.00, with a mean of .88.

Imitation

Figure 4 indicates that imitative responding increased for both subjects in training and generalization settings with the onset of training.

Social interaction

Figure 5 illustrates the rate per minute for Subjects 1 and 2 of prompted and nonprompted social interaction responses in training sessions and nonprompted social interaction responses in generalization sessions. Both subjects showed

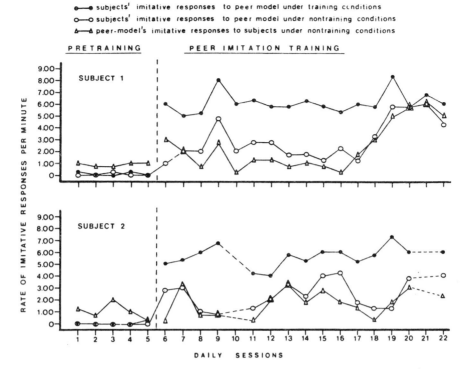

Figure 4. Rate per minute of handicapped children's imitation of nonhandicapped children under training and nontraining conditions; and nonhandicapped children's imitation of handicapped children under nontraining conditions.

increased rates of positive social interaction following training.

Negative social interaction from the subjects to the peer-model and from the peer-model to the subjects in training and generalization sessions occurred rarely. When such behavior occurred, it did not exceed 1.0 per minute and thus is not reported graphically.

The peer-model's rates of positive social interaction with Subjects 1 and 2 are depicted in Figure 5. A steady increase in social interaction under generalization conditions was demonstrated toward each subject as training progressed.

GENERAL DISCUSSION

As in previous research (Apolloni, et al., 1977; Cooke, et al., in press; Guralnick, 1976), it was only after the implementation of specific training that each of the retarded subjects began to demonstrate the desired imitation. The results of the present study clearly indicated that educational environments could be engineered wherein preschool retarded children reliably imitated the free-play and material use behavior of normally developing peers. The subjects in both experiments responded in a similar fashion to the training procedure, demonstrating stable increases in their rates of imitating nonretarded peer-models.

The most rigorous test of any behavior modification program is whether behavioral gains established in training settings generalize to environments where they are not directly reinforced. The increases in each subject's rate of imitation under nontraining conditions concomitant with acquisition of imitation during training indicate that the training gains did generalize. Comparing gains in imitative behavior across the two experiments, it was evident that the subjects in Experiment 2 demonstrated substantially larger increases under generalization conditions. Several factors may have accounted for this difference. One factor

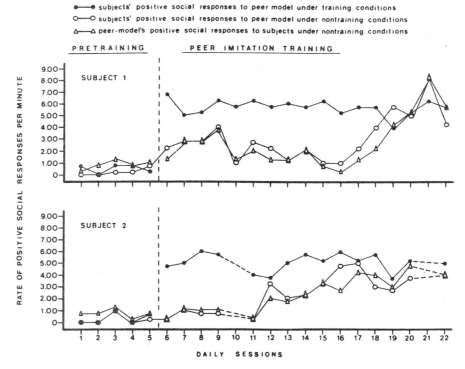

Figure 5. Rate per minute of handicapped children's social responses to nonhandicapped children under training and nontraining conditions; and nonhandicapped children's social responses to handicapped children under nontraining conditions.

may have been the difference in training activities. In Experiment 1, the activity of the peer-models was often noted to center around a set of building blocks. Retarded subjects typically did not possess the fine motor skills necessary to play with these materials on the level that was demonstrated by the peer-models. In Experiment 2, the materials and training activities were such that the retarded subjects could more easily perform with success.

Another factor promoting generalized imitation in Experiment 2 may have been the smaller number of children present in training and generalization settings. The relatively less complex free-play setting for Experiment 2 may have facilitated the establishment of peer stimulus control over the subjects' imitative behavior. Finally, clinical observation of Experiment 1 by the investigators led them to believe that the large discrepancy in behavioral sophistication between the retarded subjects (mean CA, 37 months) and peer-models (mean CA, 53 months) made the retarded subjects less desirable playmates for the peer-models and, hence, made this match of peer-models and target subjects less likely to produce generalized imitation. Generalized gains in Experiment 2 may have been facilitated by using a peer-model closer in developmental functioning level to the retarded subjects.

Another possible effect of the relatively close developmental functioning levels of the subjects and the peer-model in Experiment 2 may have been the substantial imitation of retarded subjects by the peer-model. While this "reverse" imitation demonstrated by the peer-model in Experiment 2 may be cause for concern, the investigators observed no instances in which a peer-model in either experiment imitated an undesirable behavior pattern of a retarded subject.

Baseline assessments of rates of social interaction between four of the five retarded subjects and their peer-models in these experiments, as well as evidence from other investigations (Allen et al., 1972; Karnes, Teska, & Hodgins, 1970), indicate that "integrated" may be a misnomer for many educational settings containing both handicapped and nonhandicapped children. The present data on the effects of peer-imitation training between retarded subjects and peer-models suggest that increased positive social intraction may be a beneficial side effect. It is hoped that the results of future research, together with the early findings reviewed and reported in the present work, may soon offer empirically substantiated procedures for educators charged with delivering services to preschool children in integrated settings.

References

Allen, K. E., Benning, P. M., & Drummond, T. W. Integration of normal and handicapped children in a behavior modification preschool: A case study. In G. Semb (Ed.), *Behavior analysis and education.* Lawrence, Kans.: University of Kansas Press, 1972.

Apolloni, T., & Cooke, T. P. Integrated programming at the infant, toddler, and preschool age levels. In M. Guralnick (Ed.), *Early Intervention and the Integration of Handicapped and Nonhandicapped Children.* Baltimore: University Park Press, 1977.

Apolloni, T., Cooke, S. R., & Cooke, T. P. Establishing a normal peer as a behavioral model for developmentally delayed toddlers. *Perceptual and Motor Skills,* 1977, *44,* 231–141.

Bricker, D. D., & Bricker, W. A. Toddler research and intervention project report: Year II. IMRID *Behavioral Science Monograph No. 21, Institute on Mental Retardation and Intellectual Development.* Nashville: George Peabody College, 1972.

Cooke, T. P., Cooke, S. R., & Apolloni, T. Developing nonretarded toddlers as verbal models for retarded classmates. *Child Study Journal,* in press.

Guralnick, M. J. The value of integrating handicapped and nonhandicapped preschool children. *American Journal of Orthopsychiatry,* 1976, *42,* 236–245.

Karnes, M. B., Teska, J. A., & Hodgins, A. S. The effects of four programs of classroom intervention on the intellectual and language development of 4-year-old disadvantaged children. *American Journal of Orthopsychiatry,* 1970, *40,* 58–76.

Snyder, L., Apolloni, T., & Cooke, T. P. Integrated settings at the early childhood level: The role of nonretarded peers. *Exceptional Children,* 1977, *43,* 262–266.

Strain, P. S., Cooke, T. P., & Apolloni, T. *Teaching exceptional children: Assessing and modifying social behavior.* New York: Academic, 1976.

Ulman, J. D., & Sulzer-Azaroff, B. Multielement baseline design in educational research. In E. Ramp and G. Semb (Eds.), *Behavior analysis: Areas of research and application.* Englewood Cliffs, N.J.: Prentice-Hall, 1975.

Wynne, S., Ulfelder, L. S., & Dakof, G. *Mainstreaming and early childhood education for handicapped children: Review and implications of research.* Washington, D.C.: Division of Innovation and Development, BEH-USOE, January 1975.

Instructional Modeling and the Development of Visual-and Verbal-Mediation Skills by TMR Children

Larry E. Greeson
Miami University

Ken G. Jens
University of North Carolina

A study-recall paired-associate (PA) learning task was administered to 40 TMR children under one of four instructional-modeling conditions: imagery, verbal mediation, imagery and verbal mediation, and a control condition. On one-half of the PA-learning study trials, the children were provided modeled mediating responses (connective pictures and/or sentences) and on the other trials no model was provided. The children's use of mediating responses on study trials was evaluated as was their recall performance. Each instructional-modeling condition resulted in more effective mediator use and better recall than the control condition. Verbal-mediation training was more effective than instruction in the use of visual imagery. Generation of mediators was most apparent when youngsters were first provided with models and then required to generate their own mediating responses. Gains in mediator use and recall were retained over a period of several days.

Psychologists and educators have long been concerned with the cognitive functioning of mentally retarded children and adults (e.g., Allen, 1973; Haywood, 1970; Robinson & Robinson, 1976) and conceptual problems incurred by this population have been interpreted in many ways. One of the most basic and recurring problems concerns the ability of retarded children and adults to perceive, represent, and deal symbolically with various aspects of their environment, i.e., through the use of symbolic-mediation processes.

Allen and his colleagues (Allen, 1969; Allen & Jones, 1967), using a psychometric approach, have indicated that mentally retarded persons incur problems in conceptualizing that result from an impairment of their visual-perceptual ability. Inhelder (1968), employing Piaget's theoretical framework, has interpreted the conceptual problems of mentally retarded persons in terms of "primacy of perception." That is, the retarded child or adult seems bound to features of the immediate perceptual environment rather than its more abstract conceptual features. Inhelder and Allen's work leads to the logical conclusion that there is a deficit in the ability of retarded persons to employ symbolic processes to represent and deal with meaningful aspects of their environment.

Associative-learning theorists, using a somewhat different experimental approach, have identified what they term a "mediation deficiency" on the part of retarded individuals (Goulet, 1968; Reese, 1962). While nonretarded children and adults are generally able to employ verbal or other modes of symbolic functioning to facilitate performance on learning and memory tasks, retarded persons are often unable to employ symbolic-mediation processes in a like manner (Goulet, 1968).

Goulet (1968) has indicated that the use of verbal mediation by retarded persons may be improved through instruction. Moreover, the influence of instruction on the use of mediation processes by retarded

This research was supported in part by a Georgia State University, School of Education Faculty Research Grant to the first author. We are appreciative of help provided by personnel of the Atlanta public schools, especially at the C. W. Hill Elementary School, where this study was conducted.

persons has recently been extended to the area of mental imagery (Taylor, Josberger, & Knowlton, 1972; Yarmey & Bowen, 1972; Zupnick & Meyer, 1975). Zupnick and Meyer's study is of particular significance in that it demonstrated long-term transfer effects as well as the immediate facilitation of associative learning as a function of instruction in the use of mental imagery.

The aforementioned studies have important implications for the educational and cognitive development of retarded persons; however, a number of questions remain largely unanswered. One important question concerns the retarded persons employed in mediated associative-learning studies. As Goulet (1968) has indicated, most associative-learning studies conducted with retarded individuals have employed adults as subjects and little is known regarding children. Moreover, most studies have used educable mentally retarded (EMR) persons as subjects, and little information is available concerning the associative-learning skills of trainable mentally retarded (TMR) children. That which is available offers conflicting evidence regarding TMR children's ability for associative learning. Milgram (1968) found that TMR children were unable to utilize a mediation process to facilitate learning, while Gordon and Baumeister (1971) ascertained that mediational processes could be facilitative for learning in youngsters functioning in that range.

A second question concerns the nature of symbolic functioning in retarded persons. Many studies have investigated the effects of verbal-mediation processes on learning and memory performance. Little is known, however, about the comparative development of imaginal- and verbal-mediation processes in retarded children. Such children may be deficient in the development of mental imagery as well as verbal-mediation processes. It is also possible that imaginal-mediation processes may provide an alternative mode of coding, representing, and organizing the environment for retarded children (see Yarmey & Bowen, 1972; Zupnick & Meyer, 1975). If this is the case, it would seem worthwhile to develop concrete imaginal-conceptual skills in retarded children—skills related closely to their immediate perceptual environment—as well as more abstract conceptual skills of a verbal nature.

A third question concerns the specific factors governing the development of imaginal- and verbal-mediation processes in retarded children. Previous research has indicated that one method of developing complex cognitive skills in children and adults with learning problems is through the application of modeling techniques (Bandura, 1969). Systematically designed conceptual and language-development programs, based on modeling and social-learning procedures, have been found to result in the rapid acquisition of learning sets and significant increments in the measured IQ scores of institutionalized retarded children (Jacobson, Kellogg, Greeson, & Bernal, 1973; Bernal, Jacobson, Lopez, & Greeson, Note 1). Furthermore, Ross, Ross, and Downing (1973) have provided evidence that mediational skills can be developed in EMR children through observational learning. The present study was designed to extend findings concerning modeling and cognitive development to include the development of imaginal- and verbal-mediation skills in TMR children.

Method

Subjects

Subjects for this study were 40 children enrolled in a public-school special-education program for TMR students in Atlanta, Georgia. Their mean chronological age (CA) was 11 years, 2 months (11–2), with a range extending from 6–6 to 14–7, and mean IQ (Stanford-Binet Intelligence Scale, Form L–M or Slosson Intelligence Scale) was 48.86, with a range from 34 to 61. Subjects were randomly assigned to one of three instructional-modeling conditions—imagery, verbal mediation, combined imagery and verbal mediation, or control. Mean CAs, mental ages (MAs), and IQs did not differ significantly among these groups.

Materials

A paired-associate (PA) learning task was employed, comprised of concrete familiar items chosen from primer level reading books. Item pairs were named by the experimenter and presented visually as 8 × 12 cm line drawings on 20.5 × 28 cm paper. Three practice pairs were used: rabbit–flower, shirt–apple, and balloon–key. The item pairs for the PA-learning task were: flag–candle, boat–tree, clock–umbrella, house–ball, and wagon–sun. An item-familiarization booklet containing line drawings of the individual items was also constructed in order to give the children an initial experience in naming and drawing the items prior to administration of the PA-learning task.

2. INSTRUCTION

Procedure

The experiment was divided into three parts—item familiarization, instructional modeling, and PA learning. The item-familiarization period took place prior to instructional modeling and PA learning and was identical for all of the youngsters. The instructional-modeling and PA-learning periods were varied systematically, according to differences in the experimental conditions to which the children were assigned.

Item Familiarization. During item familiarization the youngsters were asked to name and draw both practice and PA-learning items as they appeared randomly in the item-familiarization booklet. If necessary, two naming and drawing trials were administered; this period also provided time for establishing rapport with each child. Responses obtained during item familiarization served as a guide for evaluating responses obtained during the PA-learning task. Item familiarization also served as a method of screening children who were unable to draw and name, or learn how to draw and name, the PA items. Four children were replaced with alternates for this reason. The item-familiarization period was approximately 10 minutes in duration.

Instructional modeling. During instructional modeling, the practice PA items were presented as a "guessing game" and the children participating were given instructions regarding how to remember which items went together. Each child was told that he would be given a "trick for remembering" the item pairs. Children in the imagery instructional-modeling condition were told that they could remember the pairs better by drawing pictures that put the PA items together (e.g., picture of a rabbit holding a flower). Youngsters in the verbal-mediation/instructional-modeling condition were told that they could remember better by making up sentences putting the items together (e.g., "The rabbit is holding the flower"). Those in the combined imagery and verbal-mediation/instructional-modeling condition were shown how to use both pictures and sentences to help remember the PA-learning items. Mediating responses (pictures and/or verbal sentences connecting each of the three PA practice pairs) were modeled by the experimenter, and youngsters in the appropriate groups were given active practice in generating pictorial and/or syntactical mediators following instructional modeling. Control subjects were given rote rehearsal instructions, wherein they were told to name the items and draw them side-by-side. The instructional-modeling period was approximately 15 to 20 minutes in duration.

Associative learning. An individually paced study–recall PA-learning procedure was employed. PA-learning study trials were initiated in which item pairs were presented pictorially and labeled by the experimenter with the children then being asked to put the items together in pictures and/or sentences, depending on the particular condition to which they were assigned. Study-trial performance was evaluated on the basis of the number of mediating responses (connective pictures or sentences) generated. During recall, children in all conditions were asked to name or draw (their choice) the correct response items as each stimulus item was presented. Performance was evaluated in terms of the number of correct recall responses given.

The PA-learning task was administered in two five-trial sessions that differed with regard to the presence or absence of instructional modeling during the PA-study trials. During one five-trial session, the experimenter modeled mediating responses connecting the item pairs before the youngsters attempted to mediate the item pairs. In the other five-trial session, youngsters were required to generate their own mediating responses without the benefit of a modeled response. All children took part in both the conditions where mediators were experimenter modeled and self-generated, including the children in the control group who were shown a simple rehearsal strategy rather than one of the mediational strategies. Order of presentation was varied with half of the children experiencing the experimenter-modeling condition prior to being asked to generate their own mediators and half generating their own mediators before being provided an experimenter model. Each PA-learning session lasted approximately 30 to 45 minutes. There was a 3- to 10-day lapse (mean 5.95) between the two sessions for each of the children participating in these conditions.

Results

Procedures utilized in this study enabled an analysis of two between- and two within-groups factors. Between-groups factors were instructional modeling (imagery, verbal mediation, imagery and verbal mediation, no modeling) and order of session presentation (experimenter modeled/ subject generated vs. subject generated/ experimenter modeled). The two within-groups factors were experimenter modeled vs. subject generated mediators and trials.

TABLE 1

MEANS AND STANDARD DEVIATIONS (SDs) OF THE NUMBER OF MEDIATORS USED AND CORRECT RECALL RESPONSES[a] GIVEN AS A FUNCTION OF INSTRUCTIONAL MODELING

	Mediators used		Correct recall responses	
Instructional modeling condition[b]	Mean	SD	Mean	SD
Imagery	27.40	19.45	22.80	15.40
Verbal mediation	43.10	19.45	32.80	17.30
Imagery and verbal mediation	42.50	12.96	32.50	14.82
No modeling	—	—	16.10	11.69

[a] Maximum possible score for mediator use and recall performance was 50.0.
[b] $N = 10$ in each condition.

Mediator Use

The mean number of mediators utilized by children for whom the use of imagery, verbal mediation, or combined imagery and verbal mediation were modeled was significantly greater than for the control group, which did not have access to a model (Newman-Keuls $ps < .05$). The number of mediators used by children in the modeling conditions also increased significantly across PA-study trials ($F = 22.85$, $3/32$ df, $p < .001$).

As is apparent from Table 1, the verbal-mediation condition was considerably more effective in promoting mediation than was the imagery condition (Newman-Keuls $p < .05$). The difference in the mean number of mediators used under the verbal-mediation condition and the combined imagery- and verbal-mediation condition was not significant. This finding suggests that the addition of instruction in the use of imaginal mediators did not significantly enhance the facilitative effect shown for the verbal condition with regard to mediator use.

Recall Performance

Recall of items learned as PAs was significantly enhanced through the use of instructional modeling ($F = 2.86$, $3/32$ df, $p < .05$). Conditions in which verbal or a combination of verbal and imaginal mediators were used by subjects resulted in substantially better recall than did the use of imaginal mediators alone or no mediators (control condition). However, when subjected to the Newman-Keuls method of multiple comparisons, recall scores did not differ significantly among any of the four groups.

As would be expected, recall performance showed significant improvement across trials for subjects in all conditions ($F = 11.98$, $4/128$ df, $p < .001$).

Significant main effects of condition (modeling vs. generating–mediating response) and order of condition presentation were not found. However, a significant Condition × Order interaction effect was in

evidence for recall performance ($F = 18.29$, $1/32$ df, $p < .001$). As can be seen in Table 2, providing children with mediators prior to requiring them to generate their own mediating responses resulted in substantially more effective recall performance than did requiring them to generate their own mediators prior to providing them with experimentally generated mediating responses.

TABLE 2

MEAN NUMBER OF THE CORRECT RECALL RESPONSES GIVEN PER TRIAL AS A FUNCTION OF MEDIATOR CONDITION AND ORDER OF SESSION PRESENTATION

	Condition[a]			
	Experimenter modeled (EM)		Subject generated (SG)	
Order	Mean	SD	Mean	SD
EM/SG	2.50	1.79	3.06	1.80
SG/EM	2.58	1.75	1.93	1.68

[a] $N = 20$ in each condition.

Retention

In an attempt to evaluate retention, a repeated-measures analysis of variance was performed on the youngsters' recall scores on the last trial of Session 1 and the first trial of Session 2 of the PA-learning task. No significant difference in their performance was in evidence between those trials. Taken in conjunction with the overall trials effect, this is indicative that the children not only learned but also retained the PA items over a period of several days. In addition, PA-mediator use did not change significantly from the end of Session 1 to the beginning of Session 2. Thus, instructional-modeling procedures, as employed in this study, were apparently effective in developing relatively long-term mediational strategies as well as recall performance for the aforementioned TMR youngsters. These findings must be qualified, however, since a Condition × Trial interaction effect was not obtained. Thus, there was indication that all subjects, including the control group, were able to retain the PA items equally well.

Discussion

The findings of this investigation provide considerable support for the hypothesis that imagery and verbal mediation used in conjunction with instructional modeling result in effective mediator use and recall facilitation for public-school TMR children. Each instructional-modeling condition resulted in substantially greater mediator use and recall performance than did the control-instruction condition.

In addition, it was found that the verbal-mediation condition resulted in significantly more effective mediator use and recall facilitation than did the imagery condition. These findings were somewhat contrary to expectations. It was assumed that TMR children would be functioning on a relatively concrete conceptual level, one that would lend itself more to the generation of mental images (i.e., pictures) than to more abstract mediational responses of a verbal nature. One possible explanation for this finding may be that the children have engaged frequently in language-development activities, while the development of imaginal-mediation processes has been left somewhat to chance. Another explanation may be that requiring subjects in the imagery condition to draw pictures connecting the PA items may have inhibited recall performance by focusing attention on drawing skills per se, rather than the task at hand. Whatever the explanation, youngsters participating in the present study demonstrated both verbal- and imaginal-conceptual skills not generally associated with the traditional stereotype of TMR children.

We expected that TMR children would be unable to use mediating responses to facilitate recall without the aid of experimenter-provided models. However, children who were given a brief period of instructional modeling prior to administration of the PA-learning task demonstrated greater recall than control subjects when mediators were subject-generated as well as when they were provided by the experimenter, regardless of order of trial presentation. Ross et al. (1973) have indicated that EMR children may be induced to use PA-learning mediation strategies through observational learning as well as through direct instructional training. It appears that both of these factors may have been operating in this study as well.

While neither main effect was significant, a relatively strong Order of Presentation × Source of Mediator interaction effect provided support for the contention that order of presentation plays an important role in TMR children's ability to recall mediated PA items. While each order resulted in moderately effective recall on the experimenter provided trials, the experimenter-modeled/self-generated order was considerably more effective in facilitating recall on the subject-generated trials of the PA task. Thus, providing TMR children with concrete models of mediating responses on early trials and requiring them to generate their own mediating responses on later trials was particularly effective in promoting subject-generated mediator use.

Theoretically, the present study demonstrated that a social-learning conception of the development of imaginal and verbal mediation processes in TMR children is an acceptable one. Also, the present findings provide an indication that TMR children are capable, under appropriate instructional-training conditions, of utilizing complex conceptual skills of a PA-learning nature.

Educationally, the present findings support the contention that providing children with models and active practice in the generation and use of mediation processes prior to expecting them to generate their own mediators is a highly effective method of instruction, one that can result in effective mediator use and recall facilitation for TMR children attending public schools.

Direct and Vicarious Effects of Social Praise on Mentally Retarded Preschool Children's Attentive Behavior

PHILLIP S. STRAIN
Nashville, Tennessee

JAMES E. PIERCE
University of North Carolina, Chapel Hill

The purpose of this study was to examine the effects of social praise on the attentive behavior of reinforced and nonreinforced children. Two pairs of mentally retarded preschool boys served as subjects. Employing a reversal design, one child from each pair was differentially reinforced for attending to manipulative toys. The results revealed that: (a) The intervention procedure increased the attentive behavior of the target subjects. (b) Nonreinforced subjects also increased their attentive behavior during both reinforcement conditions. (c) This "spillover" of reinforcement effect was transient, as the nontarget subjects' level of attentive behavior decelerated during the final half of each 20-day reinforcement period.

Applied research on vicarious reinforcement effects has shown repeatedly that positive consequences applied to target subjects for desirable behavior increase similar behavior in nearby peers who are not reinforced directly (Christy, 1975; Drabman & Lahey, 1974; Kazdin, 1973; Kazdin, Silverman, & Sittler, 1975; Strain, Shores, & Kerr, 1976). These studies indicate that teachers may develop time- and cost-effective procedures for increasing desirable behavior in several children by: (a) discriminating which students' behavior repertoire suggests that direct consequation of behavior is required; and (b) implementing direct reinforcement procedures on these children with the expectation that nearby students who show evidence of imitative skills and a history of being reinforced by the consequent events currently delivered to target subjects will improve through vicarious reinforcement effects.

A question of considerable theoretical and practical significance that remains unanswered is whether behavior changes attributable to "spillover" effects represent a durable phenomenon, durability being defined as the maintenance of behavior change across time. The primary intent of the present study was to provide a long-term assessment of social reinforcement effects on the appropriate behavior of nontarget children.

METHOD

Subjects and Setting

Four mentally retarded preschool-age boys, ranging in age from 42 to 53 months and in IQ from 37-51 on the Stanford-Binet (Form L-M) served as subjects. The boys and their six classmates were enrolled in a private treatment center in suburban Washington, D. C. The four subjects were selected randomly to participate. The boys were grouped into pairs (Danny and Robbie; Ricky and Tom). Danny and Robbie (Pair 1) sat side by side at a large work table in one corner of the classroom, while Ricky and Tom (Pair 2) occupied a similar space in another corner of the room. During experimental periods, none of the other children were seated within 2.7m of the subjects. Within each pair, one child (Danny and Ricky) was assigned randomly to receive direct social praise for attentive behavior. Robbie and Tom never received social praise for attentive behavior. Two student teachers, one for each pair, served as reinforcing agents.

Observational Procedures

Observations of student teacher and subject behavior were conducted each day at 10:00 to 10:15 AM for Pair 1 and from 10:35 to 10:50 AM for Pair 2. Each pair with the student teacher was observed for 25 scoring intervals. Each interval was divided into 10 seconds for observing and 2 seconds for recording. Two observers for each pair sat .9m behind and directly between the boys. Child behaviors were scored as either attentive or inattentive. To be scored as attentive, a child had to be sitting in his seat and working with fine motor equipment for the full 10-second interval. Each day, both boys in each pair were given an identical assortment of manipulative toys with which to play. These included a stacking ring, two 4-piece puzzles, stringing thread and 10 beads, and a set of 10 stacking blocks. The behavior of the reinforcing agents was scored simultaneously with the behavior of the children. The frequency of student teacher delivered verbal praise contingent upon attentive behavior was scored by placing a check mark in the interval during which this event occurred.

Experimental Conditions

Each pair of subjects was exposed to the following order of experimental conditions; however, the conditions began on different days for each pair. All experimental sessions were begun by having the student teacher distribute the fine motor equipment and instruct each boy that it was time to play with these toys.

Baseline I. Attentive behavior was recorded for each child in a given pair without invoking contingencies. The initial baseline condition was in effect 8 days for Danny and Robbie and 16 days for Ricky and Tom. The student teachers sat in front of each pair of subjects, but they did not reinforce any attentive behavior.

Reinforcement of Attention I. On the ninth day of the study, Danny began to receive social praise for attentive behavior. For every two consecutive intervals of attentive behavior, the student teacher delivered social praise, "Danny, you're working nicely." The student teacher was cued visually by one of the observers when two consecutive intervals of attentive behavior had been scored. This phase lasted 20 days for Danny and Robbie. For Ricky and Tom, this phase began on day 17 and continued for 20 days. Here, an identical schedule of social reinforcement was delivered to Ricky.

Baseline II. This phase replicated the procedures in operation during the initial baseline period. This condition lasted 11 days for Pair 1 and 7 days for Pair 2. No social reinforcement was delivered to any subject throughout this phase.

Reinforcement of Attention II. This phase replicated the procedures in operation during the initial reinforcement condition. Again, the phase remained in effect for 20 days for both pairs of subjects.

RESULTS

Reliability

Interobserver reliability was calculated on each day of the study. Reliability percentages were tabulated by dividing the total number of intervals of agreement by the total number of intervals of agreement and disagreement, then multiplying by 100. For each behavior reported, reliability ranged from 88 to 100%, with a mean of 95%.

Student Teacher Social Reinforcement

During Baseline I and Baseline II, no praise events were delivered to any of the subjects. The nontarget subjects in the study, Robbie and Tom, never received teacher praise for attentive behavior throughout the course of the study. During the first reinforcement period, Reinforcement of Attention I, Danny received a mean of 8.4 social praise events each day. Ricky received a mean of 7.7 social praise events during the identical period. In the second reinforcement phase, Reinforcement of Attention II, Danny received an average of 8.2 praise events each day, while Ricky received an average of 7.5 social praise events during this period.

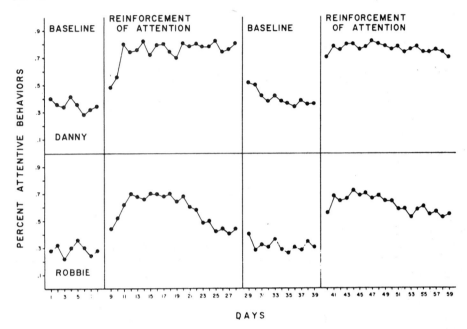

Figure 1. Daily percent of intervals scored as attentive for Danny and Robbie across all experimental conditions.

Target Subject Behavior

The top portion of Figure 1 and the top portion of Figure 2 portray the daily percent of observation intervals scored as attentive for Danny (Figure 1) and Ricky (Figure 2). During the initial Baseline I phase, both target subjects emitted a low, stable amount of attentive behavior. Figure 1 indicates that Danny's mean attentive behavior in this phase was 36%. For Ricky, attentive behaviors were observed, on the average, during 38% of the intervals. When social reinforcement procedures began for each boy, their attentive behavior increased immediately and maintained a stable, high level throughout the Reinforcement of Attention I phase. Attentive behaviors averaged 80% and 84% for Danny and Ricky, respectively. The termination of reinforcement procedures during Baseline II produced an immediate deceleration in the level of attentive behavior emitted by Danny and Ricky. For this phase, attentive behavior averaged 42% and 38% for Danny and Ricky, respectively. When the experimental contingency was again imposed during the Reinforcement of Attention II phase, attentive behavior by both Danny and Ricky increased rapidly and maintained a stable level across this 20-day period. Attentive behavior averaged 79% for Danny and 82% for Ricky during this phase.

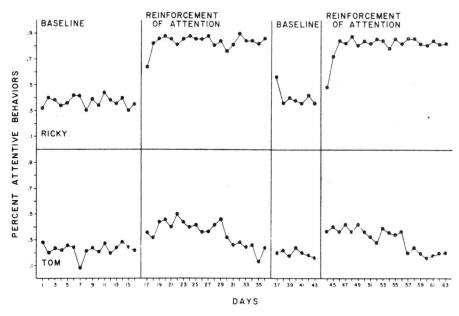

Figure 2. Daily per cent of intervals scored as attentive for Ricky and Tom across all experimental conditions.

Nontarget Subject Behavior

The initiation and termination of reinforcement procedures applied to Danny and Ricky had reliable effects on the attentive behaviors of their partners, Robbie and Tom. As the lower portions of Figures 1 and 2 indicate, Robbie and Tom engaged in a stable, low amount of attentive behavior during the initial Baseline I condition. Attentive behaviors averaged 31% for Robbie and 26% for Tom during this period. When the contingency was applied to Danny and Ricky during the Reinforcement of Attention I phase, Robbie's attentive behavior increased to a mean of 61%. However, as reflected in the bottom portion of Figure 1, the vicarious reinforcement or "spillover" effects clearly diminished across the 20-day period. For example, attentive behavior during the second 5-day segment of this phase averaged 69% as compared to 47% across the final five days of this phase. A similar behavior pattern was evident for Tom. As shown in the lower portion of Figure 2, contingency procedures applied to Ricky during the Reinforcement of Attention I phase resulted in a concomitant increase in Tom's attentive behavior. Across the 20-day period, attentive behavior averaged 43%. This "spillover" effect diminished considerably across this phase with an average of 27% attentive behavior during the last five days, compared to an average of 42% for the second 5-day segment of the phase. When the contingency was terminated for the target subjects during the Baseline II phase, attentive behavior by Robbie and Tom declined accordingly. Attentive behavior averaged 33% and 22% for Robbie and Tom, respectively. The reinstatement of the experimental contingency for Danny and Ricky resulted once again in an increased level of attentive behavior by Robbie and Tom. Again, however, this "spillover" of reinforcement effect diminished across the 20-day Reinforcement of Attention II phase. Attentive behavior averaged 63% for Robbie and 38% for Tom across this phase. During the second 5-day period of this phase, Robbie's attentive behavior averaged 68% compared to 53% across the last five days of the phase. For Tom, attentive behaviors averaged 36% across the second 5-day period and 19% across the final five days of the Reinforcement of Attention II phase.

DISCUSSION

The major findings of this study were: (a) Contingent social praise by the student teachers increased the attentive behavior of the target subjects. (b) "Spillover" effects of social praise were noted for the nontarget subjects who increased their level of attentive behavior during both intervention periods. (c) This "spillover" effect was transient, as the nontarget subjects' level of attentive behavior diminished during the second half of each 20-day intervention phase.

Previous research (e.g., Kazdin, 1973; Kazdin, et al., 1975; Strain, et al., 1976) has shown that "spillover" effects represent a phenomenon equal in stability to direct social reinforcement effects. By extending the reinforcement phase beyond that typically employed in single-subject designs, this study shows that accelerated performance by nonreinforced subjects will diminish in the prolonged absence of direct reinforcement. This finding is consistent with the laboratory research of Bandura (1971), who repeatedly demonstrated that increased aggressive and affiliative behaviors by nonreinforced observers represent transient behavior change.

The results reported here suggest that "spillover" effects may be employed in applied settings to initiate positive behavior change by several children, but that some direct consequation is required to maintain these positive behaviors. Further research is now underway to identify the necessary level of direct reinforcement needed to maintain "spillover" effects.

References

Bandura, A. *Principles of behavior modification.* New York: Holt, 1971.

Christy, P. R. Does use of tangible rewards with individual children affect peer observers? *Journal of Applied Behavior Analysis*, 1975, *8*, 187-196.

Drabman, R. S., & Lahey, B. B. Feedback in classroom behavior modification: Effects on the target and her classmates. *Journal of Applied Behavior Analysis*, 1974, *7*, 591-598.

Kazdin, A. E. The effect of vicarious reinforcement on attentive behavior in the classroom. *Journal of Applied Behavior Analysis*, 1973, *6*, 71-78.

Kazdin, A. E., Silverman, N. A., & Sittler, J. L. The use of prompts to enhance vicarious effects of nonverbal approval. *Journal of Applied Behavior Analysis*, 1975, *8*, 279-286.

Strain, P. S., Shores, R. E., & Kerr, M. M. An experimental analysis of "spillover" effects on the social interaction of behaviorally handicapped preschool children. *Journal of Applied Behavior Analysis*, 1976, *9*, 31-40.

Improving the Sequential Memory Performance of Trainable Mentally Retarded Youngsters: Learning Strategies Approach

Clark L. Wambold, Ed.D.
University of Wisconsin-Madison

KATHY JEDLINSKI, B.D.
Janesville Public Schools
Janesville, Wis.

CLARK L. WAMBOLD, Ed.D.
University of Wisconsin-Madison

KATHY JEDLINSKI, B.S.
Janesville Public Schools
Janesville, Wis.

LOU BROWN, Ph.D.
University of Wisconsin-Madison

It is a common source of frustration for those who work with retarded persons in learning situations that the mentally retarded (MR) recall information less well than their normal peers. Rather than merely diluting the MR curriculum, special education should include particular techniques to improve information recall. One possible way to accomplish this is to translate recent findings of human learning experimentation into practical classroom procedures. Aserlind (1969) suggested the following procedures for achieving such a goal: "(a) read and understand the research as presented; (b) see the implications for classroom application; (c) create a transitional application; (d) test and refine the application; and (e) disseminate the results of this translation process" (p. 43).

Recent research suggests that at least part of poor MR recall results from a short-term memory (STM) deficit. Short-term memory is defined herein as recall within seconds, as opposed to long-term memory, which is recall over a matter of hours (Scott & Scott, 1968). According to Ellis (1970) in his recently revised memory model, the STM deficit results from a rehearsal strategy deficiency in the MR. He posited that rehearsal strategies are necessary for transferring information from primary memory (PM), a limited capacity system, to secondary memory (SM), a system which increases the amount and duration of storage. Rehearsal is necessary when the task requires storage of a greater number of items than can be handled by PM alone. Since most MR individuals do not rehearse, they typically retain only the last few items in a serial learning task. He also speculated that the rehearsal strategy deficiency may be linked to other intellectual behaviors which are typically poor for the MR. At the time of his report, Ellis (1970) was unable to detail the functions of the rehearsal mechanism other than to suggest that it involves such things as "chunking strategies, other grouping and organization devices and encoding (a transduction of information from visual to an auditory code . . .)" (p. 7).

"Improving the Sequential Memory Performance of Trainable Mentally Retarded Youngsters: A Learning Strategies Approach," C. Wambold, K. Jedlinski, L. Brown, *The Journal of Special Education*, Spring 1976. ©1976 by the Journal of Special Education.

Butterfield, Wambold, and Belmont (1973) developed the rehearsal strategy deficit hypothesis into a laboratory technique for training retarded adolescents to perform as well as normal adults on a serial learning task. This was accomplished by first observing the strategies used by normal adults on the task, then observing and comparing how the strategies of the retarded differed from those of the normals, and finally developing and training the retarded to use normal adult strategies.

The present study developed similar techniques for improving the sequential memory performance of trainable mentally retarded (TMR) youngsters in a classroom setting. Two basic learning strategies were taught—labeling and rehearsal by repetition—and the following research questions were examined:

1. Will label training alone improve the sequential memory performance of TMR youngsters?

2. Will rehearsal training (repetition) improve the sequential memory performance of TMR youngsters?

METHOD

Subjects

Three subjects (Ss), two male and one female, from a primary class for TMR participated in the present study. Individual statistics for the Ss at the beginning of the program were as follows:

S1 was 9 years–7 months of age with a full-scale score of 58 on the WISC. Anecdotal descriptions of S1's behavior, contained in his cumulative folder, included such statements as "poor motor coordination, . . . attention span is short."

S2 was 10 years–11 months of age. She had an IQ of 52 on the Stanford-Binet (Form L-M). She was described in her cumulative records as "severely delayed in speech and language development, . . . inattentive."

S3 was 8 years–5 months of age with an IQ of 43 on the Stanford-Binet (Form L-M). Anecdotal remarks describing S3 were similar to those for the above Ss.

Materials

Ten (five stimulus and five matched display) 3 × 5-inch index cards were used, with a single object drawn on or taped to each; one 3 × 5-inch green tagboard card had the word GO printed on it. The following pictures of objects were used as stimuli: stapler, quarter, dime, faucet, and safety pin.

Five cards were used as display cards to be manipulated by the Ss on a 12 × 18-inch piece of orange construction paper (playing area) having two rows of five 3 × 5-inch rectangles. Five duplicate cards were used as stimuli cards to be presented to the Ss by the teacher at timed intervals. Intervals were kept using the second hand of a wrist watch. Cereal bits and M & M candies were used as reinforcement.

Procedures

During each session the teacher and the three Ss were seated at a table in the back of the classroom while the remaining seven students in the class worked on assignments at their desks. A total of 52 sessions lasted approximately 25 min each. Conducted on successive school days, the sessions included 2 for stimulus selection and pretraining, 6 for baselining, 7 for label teaching, and 39 for rehearsal teaching.

Stimulus selection and pretraining. Stimuli for the program were selected by screening common objects until five were found that none of the three Ss could overtly label. During screening the teacher presented one of the stimuli cards and asked, "What is this?" The S's response was recorded, and the teacher proceeded to the next S and presented a different stimuli ˙ card, asking the same question. The teacher did not indicate whether or not their responses were correct. An object was selected if all of the Ss responded incorrectly on two successive presentations.

Following the stimulus selection, the five objects were used to generate random sequences of two, three, four, and five objects which would be the serial lists used in the program. For example, there were three sequences each of: two objects—faucet/dime, stapler/quarter, and safety pin/faucet (Set I); three objects—dime/stapler/faucet, quarter/safety pin/dime, and

faucet/quarter/stapler (Set II); and so on for sequences of four (Set III) and five (Set IV) objects.

After the sequences had been selected, the teacher demonstrated the use of the playing area by presenting herself with a two-object sequence. She responded after the presentation of the GO card by taking the appropriate cards from the top row of the playing area and placing them in order from left to right in the bottom row. Each S was then tested with the same two-object sequence to determine if the procedure was understood. Whether the S ordered the objects properly was not important during pretraining. As soon as the Ss had demonstrated they understood the procedures, the baseline study (B1) was conducted to determine how many of the sequences of two, three, four, and five objects the Ss could correctly duplicate without knowing the name of the objects. The five display cards were placed in the top row of the playing area. The teacher then presented at 5-sec intervals the stimulus cards, speaking the word "This" for each card of the sequence, followed by the green GO card. After presentation of the GO card, one S, while the others watched, responded by removing cards from the top row and placing them in the bottom row of the playing area in the order he remembered seeing them. The teacher then recorded the response with a plus (+) if correct, or with a minus (−) and the order given by the S if incorrect. No indication of correctness or reinforcement was given at this time. The turn was then passed to the next S. The baseline was completed when each S had responded to all sequences of two, three, four, and five objects.

Label teaching. Labels were taught for the five objects using the 3 × 5-inch stimulus cards. The presentation of the stimulus cards followed the same format as the baseline study, except that during this teaching session correctness was indicated and reinforcement was offered. If an S responded with the correct label for the object stimulus card, he was praised (e.g., "yes," "that's right," "good _____"), given a cereal bit or M & M

2. INSTRUCTION

candy, and the turn them passed to the next S. If the S did not respond or responded incorrectly, the teacher would model the correct response, saying "No, this is not a _____. This is a _____. Now you say _____." The S was praised for imitating verbally the correct label, and the turn passed to the next S. If the S did not respond correctly to the first model, a second model was given and then, regardless of the response, the turn passed to the next S. A trial was completed when each S had responded to each of the five stimulus cards once. Only the Ss first response to a stimulus card was recorded; responses to modeled labels were not recorded.

At this time a second baseline study (B2) was conducted to determine whether teaching the labels alone had any effect on the Ss' performance of the sequential ordering task. No reinforcement was used.

Rehearsal teaching. During this phase of the study Ss were instructed to use a cumulative rehearsal or building strategy. Teaching began with a two-item sequence and an item was added through five each time an S achieved a criterion of three consecutive correct responses. The cumulative rehearsal strategy involved repeating the names of all previous items as many times as possible during the successive interitem intervals. For example, in the sequence A–B–C–D the teacher presents the A card for a 5-sec interval, places the A card face down, presents the B card and exposes it for 5 sec, places it face down, and repeats the procedure through all items. During the 5-sec interval and until the next item appears, the S repeats as many times as possible the items which have previously been presented. Following the last item, the teacher presents the GO card and the S responds by attempting to place the display cards in the correct sequence. Throughout this phase of the study if the S responded by placing the stimulus cards in the proper order, he was praised and given a cereal bit or an M & M candy. The teacher recorded the response and proceeded to the next S. If the response was incorrect, the teacher recorded the response and then dem-

onstrated the rehearsal strategy and the correct response. The S then imitated the teacher's model and attempted to place the display cards in the proper sequential order in the bottom row of the playing area. If, at this point, the response was correct, the S was praised for rehearsing but not given a tangible reinforcer and the turn passed to the next S. If the response was incorrect, the modeling procedure was demonstrated again. The S made another attempt at placing the cards in correct order. A correct response resulted in praise and an incorrect response resulted in the teacher saying, "I'm sorry, that's not right." the turn was then passed to the next S. This procedure was followed until a trial was completed, i.e., each S had a chance to respond to three sequences. Nine responses were required to complete a trial. Three consecutive trials with all responses correct were required for moving to the next step of the program.

After criteria had been met for Set I, a baseline study (B3) was conducted for all sequences with reinforcement for correct rehearsal of the sequences in Set I but not for those of the other sets. The same procedure was followed for the remaining sets until S reached criterion on a five-item sequence (Set IV) and a final baseline was administered. The following summarizes the steps of the program:

1. Stimulus selection and pretraining
2. Baseline 1 (B1)
3. Teach labels
4. Baseline 2 (B2)
5. Teach Set I (two-object sequence)
6. Baseline 3 (B3)
7. Teach Set II (three-object sequence)
8. Baseline 4 (B4)
9. Teach Set III (four-object sequence)
10. Baseline 5 (B5)
11. Teach Set IV (five-object sequence)
12. Baseline 6 (B6)

RESULTS AND DISCUSSION

The results of the serial position data of the initial baseline (B1) and the base-

line following label teaching (B2) are summarized in Figure 1 for the three Ss. Each of the baselines consist of nine responses (three per subject) per serial position. There is little difference between the initial baseline and the baseline which followed label teaching, which suggests that labels alone were not sufficient to improve the Ss' performance. They were necessary, however, since without labels the objects would be difficult to rehearse.

The rehearsal training phase of the present study consisted of teaching the youngsters to cumulatively rehearse the stimulus objects. The use of rehearsal was shaped by first presenting two, then three, then four, and finally five items. An additional item was added each time an S reached a criterion of three successive correct responses. The trials to criterion for two (Set I), three (Set II), four (Set III), and five (Set IV) items were 13, 17, 22, and 20, respectively. The results of the baselines which followed each rehearsal-teaching set are shown in Figure 2. The Ss' performance improved on each succeeding baseline as items were added. On the final baseline (B6) all Ss performed maximally.

The results of the present study are consistent with basic research efforts which suggest that: (a) the poor recall of the MR results from a rehearsal strategy deficit (Ellis, 1970); and (b) poor recall may be improved by teaching the retarded to use rehearsal strategies (Butterfield, Wambold, & Belmont, 1973).

The purpose of this study was to develop classroom techniques for improving the recall of MR youngsters. This was accomplished for the present task. There remain, however, a number of questions which must be examined to determine the lasting value of training strategies, such as those in this study. One major issue relates to the generalization and retention of trained strategies. If we are able to improve MR performance on a specific task, will the strategy carry over to subsequent similar situations? If special education is to develop a curriculum to remedy MR intellectual deficits, further applied research efforts must be undertaken in an effort to answer this question.

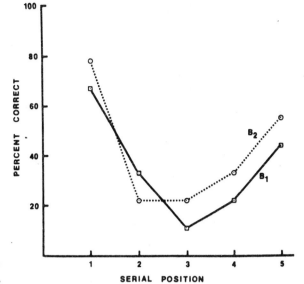

Figure 1. Percentage of correct responses over serial positions for the three *S*s prior to B1 and following B2 label teaching.

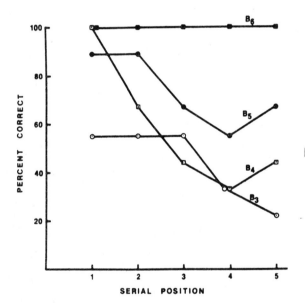

Figure 2. Percentage of correct responses over serial positions for the three *S*s following rehearsal teaching of two-item (B3), three-item (B4), four-item (B5), and five-item (B6) sequences.

References

Aserlind, L. Research: Some implications for the classroom. *Teaching Exceptional Children*, 1969, *1*, 42–54.

Butterfield, E. C., Wambold, C., & Belmont, J. M. On the theory and practice of improving short-term memory. *American Journal of Mental Deficiency*, 1973, *77*, 654–669.

Ellis, N. R. Memory processes in retardates and normal. In N. R. Ellis (Ed.), *International review of research in mental retardation* (Vol. 4). New York: Academic Press, 1970.

Scott, K. G., & Scott, M. S. Research and theory in short-term memory. In N. R. Ellis (Ed.), *International review of research in mental retardation* (Vol. 3). New York: Academic Press, 1968.

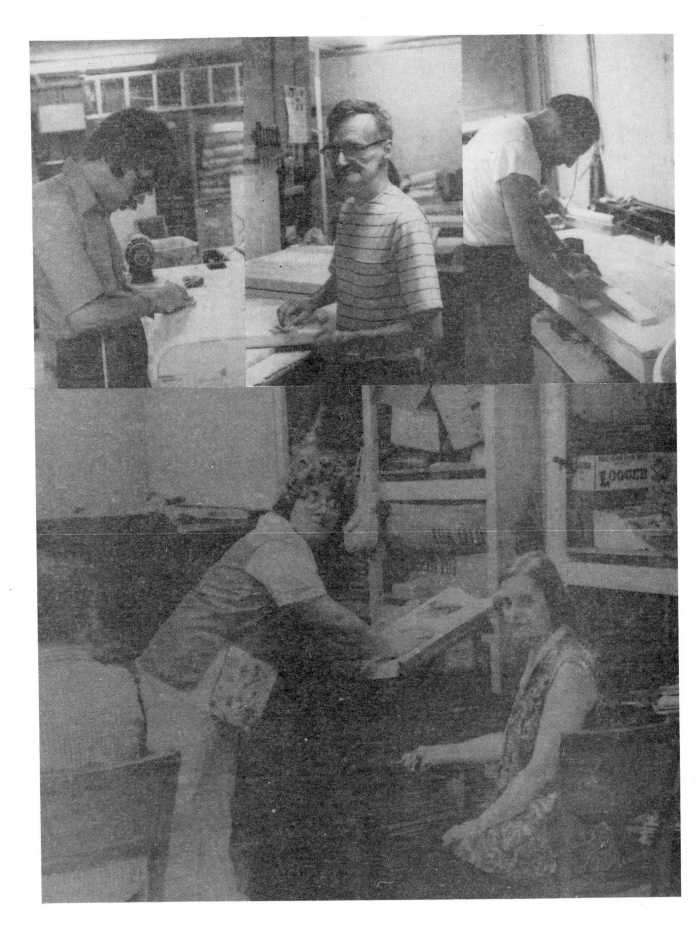

Photographs by Ann Rivellini

Assimilating the Trainable Mentally Handicapped Into Society

The trainable mentally handicapped population possesses untapped potential both in school and vocational areas. In order for these potentials to be tapped by educators, the trainable mentally handicapped must be integrated into society as much as is appropriate. It is recognized today that these people do not belong in an isolated and forgotten educational setting. Normalization and mainstreaming can do much to enhance the self-images and performances of the trainable mentally handicapped. Appropriate educational placement and meaningful vocational training are both equally important and in too many cases, lacking.

While the trainable mentally handicapped need supervision and care in many aspects of their lives, Public Law 94-142 mandates that this population be given the opportunity to reach full potential through appropriate education.

Career education affords the trainable mentally handicapped with a look beyond the traditional sheltered workshop and a possible lack of industrial challenge. Along with meaningful careers, the trainable mentally handicapped are entitled to explore appropriate leisure activities and constructive after school/work choices.

The appropriate placement of the trainable mentally handicapped into our public schools is the first step toward providing this population with the most normalized environment possible.

The trainable mentally handicapped deserve the opportunity to approach their potential in a dignified and productive manner and it is incumbent on our educational structure and society itself to insure this end.

Career Education for Trainable Mentally Retarded Youth

RALPH L. BECKER
QUENTIN WIDENER
A. Z. SOFORENKO

Abstract: A mailed survey was used to assess the type of training to which TMR youth were assigned and to identify work related problems of job failure and placement. Forty-three TMR personnel from 36 school districts in 12 states completed a 3-part questionnaire reporting data for the school period 1977–78. Trainees and incumbent workers were predominantly involved in noncompetitive subcontract job tasks. A smaller percentage were involved in competitive service occupations. Opportunities are expanding to include community competitive employment.

The U.S. Office of Education (1975) definition of career education is "the totality of experiences through which one learns about and prepares to engage in work as part of her or his way of living." Brolin (1977) defines career education as a total educational concept for systematically coordinating all school, family, and community components to facilitate each individual's potential for economic, social, and personal fulfillment. Given the above two definitions, the intent of career education is to serve as a catalyst towards the unification of educational and community systems around the central theme of work (D'Alonzo, 1977).

Application of the concept of career education for trainable mentally retarded (TMR) children has pointed up serious barriers to its fulfillment. At the present time most programs which exist in public schools are primarily for the educable mentally retarded child. Trainable children are generally trained for placement in a sheltered workshop, or, most optimistically, in sheltered community employment.

This survey has three purposes: (a) to identify and describe the kinds of problems that training personnel were currently experiencing in job training and placement of TMR youth, (b) to identify causes of job failure in the TMR worker, and (c) to identify the type of jobs and setting where TMR youth were assigned for work training or job placement.

Procedure

A three-part questionnaire was devised to gain information related to the three purposes. In part one of the questionnaire were listed 10 problem statements requiring the respondents to sort each problem into one of the five following categories:

1. A Major Problem: one that may require a great deal of time, many decisions, and a great deal of effort.
2. A Moderate Problem: one that may require considerable time, frequent decisions, and considerable effort.
3. An Average Problem: one that may require an average amount of time, decision, and effort.
4. A Minor Problem: one that may require little time, few decisions, and little effort.
5. No Problem: one that may require a minimum of time, decision, and effort.

Problem statements were developed from various sources: interviews with workshop personnel, journal and periodical articles,

Reprinted from *Education and Training of the Mentally Retarded*, Vol. 14, No. 2, April 1979, by R.L. Becker, Q. Widener, and A.Z. Soforenko, and the Council for Exceptional Children. Copyright 1979 by the Division on Mental Retardation, the Council for Exceptional Children, 1920 Association Drive, Reston, Virginia 22091.

TABLE 1

Problem Statements and Mean Values

Problem statements	Mean rating*
Obtaining community involvement, government and voluntary service agencies in meeting the needs of workshop workers	2.34
Obtaining adequate physical facilities for the TMR program such as floor space and workrooms for the workshop	2.42
Obtaining adequate transportation for workers to workshop facilities for training or employment	2.52
Having sufficient time and personnel to watch over the quality and quantity of worker-produced services and products	2.68
Obtaining skilled workshop personnel	2.69
Having adequate time for curriculum development and planning of the workshop program	2.89
Obtaining follow-up information on TMR workers after leaving the workshop facility	2.97
Retraining workers for new jobs due to mechanized procedures for accomplishing the same task or job obsolescence	3.06
Having adequate time for guidance and counseling with workshop workers	3.08
Communicating with parents and enlisting their cooperation in the workshop program	3.32

* The lower the mean rating the more serious the problem.

and local and federal government publications. A small pool of statements was developed from these sources with the final collection consisting of the 10 most frequently given statements that were appropriate for the study.

Part two of the questionnaire consisted of three statements directly under the control of the TMR worker as major reasons for failure in the world of work (D'Alonzo, 1977). Respondents were required to rank the causative statements on a forced-choice format as first, second, and third with the lower the numeral the more prevalent the reasons for job failure. In part three of the questionnaire, respondents were requested to itemize the specific jobs or job tasks and the estimated number of TMR workers assigned to that activity.

In order to determine the location of TMR programs nationwide, chief school officers in each of the 50 states were requested to forward to the project office state directories of special education listing available TMR programs, by school system, within each state. From the states reporting TMR programs, a random sample of school districts was selected and questionnaires were mailed to either administrators in charge of the TMR programs within a school system or directly to the individual named in the directory as supervisor of the school building TMR program. Replies to the questionnaire were received from 43 TMR personnel (coordina-

tors, directors, teachers, supervisors) representing 51% of the initial sample. Replies included data from 36 school districts in 12 states. The mean chronological age of TMR youth was 18 years, 6 months, and the mean IQ was 45. Replies to the questionnaire by TMR personnel gave vocational information for the 1977–78 school year.

For purposes of reporting, jobs or job types are listed under one of three classifications: (a) subcontract work—activities that are accomplished under close supervision in a workshop or sheltered work area; (b) competitive occupations—the delivery of services and nonmanufacturing activity; and (c) competitive occupations—the manufacture of goods and commodities as the main product.

Results

Problem Statements

For each of the problem statements listed in the questionnaire, respondents rated the difficulty of each statement as it applied in their program. Each problem statement was rated according to one of the five categorical positions as described. A mean rating was then determined for each of 10 statements based on the returns of 43 questionnaires.

Table 1 shows the problem statements and their mean ratings. This table shows that the major problem in training facilities is that

TABLE 2

Mean Values and Ranks of Worker Controlled Causes of Job Failure

Job failure statements	Mean rating	Rank*
Lack of appropriate social-emotional maturity to function effectively at work	1.39	1
Limited attending skills such as self-help, self-care, and expressive language	1.92	2
Lack of physical stamina and vitality sustained over a prolonged period of time	2.68	3

* The lower the rank the more serious the cause of failure.

of obtaining community involvement of government and voluntary service agencies in meeting the needs of workshop workers as the average major problem in training facilities. Respondents also indicated that obtaining adequate physical facilities for the TMR program such as floor space and workrooms in the prevocational training area and workshops was a second major problem. By contrast, communicating with parents and enlisting their cooperation in the workshop program was viewed, on the average, as the least serious problem by the same training personnel. A categorical rating of one indicated a problem was a major difficulty; a rating of five implied that it was considered as minimal or no problem. Consequently, the lower the mean rating, the more serious the problem was considered by the rater.

Job Failure Statements

Failure to be successful in the world of work can be directly attributed to (a) lack of physical stamina and vitality sustained over a prolonged period of time, (b) lack of appropriate social-emotional maturity to function effectively at work, and (c) limited attending skills such as self-help, self-care, and expressive language. Each of these conditions is under the direct control of the TMR client and may restrict his or her employability.

Respondents ranked the three job failure statements with a rank of 1 for the job condition they considered most prevalent as a cause for job failure and with a rank of 3 for the condition they considered to be least prevalent. A mean rating was established for each of the triad statements based on the 43 questionnaires.

Table 2 presents the mean ratings and ranks for each of the triad statements. Inspection of Table 2 shows that the major reported cause of client job failure is lack of appropriate social-emotional maturity to function effectively in the work situation.

In contrast, lack of physical stamina and vitality to work over a prolonged period of time was ranked as the least contributing cause of client job failure.

Job Training and Placement

In part three of the questionnaire respondents indicated the type of job or skill training and work placement attained in their TMR program. Table 3 presents data on the noncompetitive (subcontract sheltered activity) and competitive occupations from responding TMR personnel.

An estimated 60% of the job listings reported by respondents involved some type of subcontract work requiring the TMR worker to either sort, package, assemble, collate, sew,

TABLE 3

Type of Work and Job Placement of TMR Clients by Competitive and Noncompetitive Categories

Noncompetitive occupations
(Subcontract work) 60%
    Sorting
    Package*
    Assemble*
    Collate
    Sewing
    Salvage
    Light machine operations
Competitive occupations
(Service & nonmanufacturing) 39%
    Automotive and transportation
    Janitorial and building maintenance*
    Horticulture
    Clerical
    Food service*
    Laundry service
    Personal service
Competitive occupations
(Manufacturing) 1%
    Woodworking
    Ceramics
    Simple bench work*
    Light machine work

* Most frequently reported job activity within a category.

salvage, or to use light machine operations to complete the specified job. The most frequently assigned activity within this category required the incumbent worker to assemble or package a given product. An estimated 39% of the reported job placements consisted of competitive occupations that were service oriented and nonmanufacturing. Within this classification the jobs listed most frequently were in food service and janitorial/building maintenance occupations. Competitive occupations that were nonservice but primarily manufacturing or production of a commodity received the fewest job placements. An estimated 1% of the job placements reported by TMR personnel were in this classification. The most frequently listed job activity within this category was simple bench work.

Discussion and Summary

Work study and job placement personnel from 36 school districts in 12 states completed a three-part questionnaire reporting on work assignments and related issues in the vocational education of the TMR for the school period 1977–78.

The major problem areas identified in this survey point up the need for substantially more involvement by local and federal agencies in meeting training needs of TMR clients. Coupled with this lack of community and federal involvement is the specified need for additional physical facilities to operate the TMR program.

A major cause of client job failure was attributed to lack of social and emotional maturity to cope effectively at work. Frustrations brought on by the task itself, personal interactions with fellow workers and supervisors, or the interaction effect of both sources

seriously undermine the employability of this group of retarded workers.

Trainees and incumbent workers were assigned predominantly (60%) to sheltered placement involving job tasks limited to noncompetitive or subcontract activity. Trainees and incumbent workers in sheltered employment tend to spend much of their working effort in tasks requiring assembling and packaging of a wide variety of products and commodities. An estimated two-fifths (40%) of the trainees or incumbents are either being trained for or working in careers outside of sheltered employment. A large proportion of this group is employed in service occupations including food service and janitorial or building maintenance. The findings of the placement survey show that job training opportunities for TMR youth are expanding to include competitive community employment. However, in comparison to job opportunities available to educable mentally retarded (EMR) youth, there is a marked reduction in the type and kind of job placement (Becker, 1976).

References

Becker, R. L. Job training placement for retarded youth: A survey. *Mental Retardation*, 1976, *14*, 7–11.

Brolin, D. E. Career development: A national priority. *Education and Training of the Mentally Retarded*, 1977, *12*, 154–156.

D'Alonzo, B. J. Trends and issues in career education for the mentally retarded. *Education and Training of the Mentally Retarded*, 1977, *12*, 156–158.

U.S. Department of Health, Education and Welfare, Office of Education, Office of Career Education. *An introduction to career education.* Washington, D.C.: Government Printing Office, 1975.

Integration of Young TMR Children into a Regular Elementary School

Suzanne Ziegler
Donald Hambleton

SUZANNE ZIEGLER *is Research Consultant, Board of Education, Toronto, Ontario;* DONALD HAMBLETON *is Research Coordinator, Metropolitan Toronto School Board, Ontario.*

Two classes of young trainable mentally retarded (TMR) children were moved from a school for the retarded to a regular public school where they interacted with the school population daily, mainly in nonacademic (nonclassroom) situations. Their behavior at two time points during the year was compared to that of a matched group of TMR children in a school for the retarded.

Evaluation Design

The evaluation was designed to assess the effects of placing TMR children in a public school setting, primarily through direct observation and recording of the quantity and quality of interactions between retarded and nonretarded children.

As the two classes to be included in the regular school were selected prior to the initiation of evaluation, pretreatment equivalence of the experimental (integration) and contrast (segregation) groups through random assignment of children could not be achieved. Therefore, a matched group design was chosen. Variables on which children were matched included sex, chronological age, mental age, social age, etiology, language(s) spoken in the home, student's expressive and receptive language, number of siblings in the home and birth order, and socioeconomic background, based on the father's education and occupation.

As a check of the efficacy of the matching process, group means of several of the matching variables were computed (Campbell & Stanley, 1963). The experimental (integration) and contrast groups were found to be similar. For example, for IQ scores, the mean of the integrated group was 40.4; for the contrast group, the mean was 42.2. Group mean scores on sections of an adapted version of the Cain-Levine Social Competency Scale (Cain & Levine, 1963) filled out by the children's own teacher subsequent to the matching procedure, also supported group comparability.

Collection of Data

The tools developed included a behavior checklist to be used in play situations outside the classroom and an interaction analysis.

The Behavior Checklist

The checklist details the relative frequency of 13 kinds of interactions among retarded and nonretarded students. Scoring involved coding of occurrence, quality, and the source (initiator) of interactions involving the retarded children. These 13 categories, which ranged from solitary noninvolvement to cooperative interaction, were collapsed for analysis into three: *inadequate, adequate* and *extremely adequate* social behavior.

The data gathered during two time periods (December/January and April/May), showed no statistically significant differences between the experimental and contrast groups.

A comparison of total instances of aggressive, ignoring and hostile behavior by the nonretarded children in the integrated environment supports the findings of some previous studies (e.g. Hayes, 1969) that nonretarded children, contrary to commonly held beliefs, do not single out and deliberately victimize the retarded.

The Interaction Analysis

In addition to the behavior checklists, additional data was collected and subjected to an interaction analysis, to document not only frequencies of specific social behaviors, but also patterns or chains of such interactions. Tabulations of selected interaction patterns are presented in Table 1.

Interactions involving only retarded children observed at both schools were also predominantly positive in character, but included more provoked aggression and much less teaching, intervening and comforting/helping than interactions involving nonretarded and retarded children. It is important to note that retarded children not only play and converse together, but also that retarded children *help, intervene,* and *comfort,* although apparently less frequently and less effectively than nonretarded children in comparable situations.

As well as studying the interaction of retarded and nonretarded students on the playground, independent measures were used to assess how well known the retarded students were as individuals to the nonretarded children. A surprisingly large number of regular students knew the special class children, not only as a group, but individually and by name.

Conclusions

There can be little doubt that the placement of the special classes in a regular school was extremely effective in promoting interaction between the retarded and nonretarded students, and thus in providing a more normal environment for the retarded children.

References

Cain, L.F. & Levine, S. Effects of community and institutional programs on trainable mentally retarded children. *Research Monograph,* Washington DC: The Council for Exceptional Children, 1963.

Campbell, D.T. & Stanley, J.C. *Experimental and quasi-experimental designs for research.* Chicago: Rand McNally, 1963.

Hayes, G.A. The integration of the mentally retarded and non-retarded in a day camping program: A demonstration project. *Mental Retardation,* 1969, October, 14-16.

TABLE 1

Frequency of Selected Behavior Patterns
on the Playground Integration Site—35 Hours Observation

Interactions	N^1+E^2 female/female	N+E female/male	N+E male/female	N+E male/male	Total N+E
Positive					
Friendly conversation	87	44	18	51	200
Friendly physical contact	127	47	31	77	282
Game	17	5	1	2	25
Parallel play	9	8	0	6	23
Play	5	2	1	17	25
Instruct (verbal)	6	10	1	8	25
Teach skill	13	13	1	0	27
Intervene and correct	10	12	7	24	53
Reprimand	7	6	1	9	23
Comfort	10	3	1	7	21
Help	23	13	3	12	51
Total positive and/or teaching interaction	314	163	65	213	755
Negative					
Verbal aggression	1	0	1	0	2
Physical aggression (without distinction as to initiator)	11	2	1	13	27
Total aggressive interactions	12	2	2	13	29
Total interactions	326	165	67	226	784

[1] N = nonretarded children
[2] E = retarded children (experimental group)

Self Concepts of Senior TMR Students at a Semi-Integrated Setting

B. Chris Nash
Alan McQuisten

ABSTRACT. Investigators compared the self-concepts of senior TMR students attending a regular high school with TMR students at a segregated school. Structured clinical interviews were conducted with 19 students at each setting. Questions posed were based on those of Hambleton and Zieglar (1973). The semi-integration plans did not involve any special orientation of regular high school students to the needs of the retarded students. No significant differences were found, and it is suggested that even without planning of semi-integration, such placement does not adversely affect the self-concepts of TMR students.

Introduction

This study was part of an investigation into some of the effects of the placement of a senior school (age range 13–21 years) for Trainable Mentally Retarded (TMR) students in a regular high school. Such placements would be categorized as "semi-integration" using Foxcroft's (1972) definition. At a semi-integrated facility, classes of trainable retarded students occupy separate classrooms or a separate section of a regular school. Hambleton and Ziegler (1973) observed three types of "semi-integration" facilities, and noted that there were many variations among the settings.

The differences encountered in the present study seemed to represent the level of semi-integration desired by the school board and the staffs of both schools involved.

In the present case, the sharing of space was based upon an administrative decision to make use of existing available physical facilities. No special planning for semi-integration was possible and so the effects of side-by-side placement could be studied without the effect of desired specific outcomes.

Lawrence and Winschel's review of research and issues about the self-concepts of retarded students noted that there have been very few studies of the self-concepts of TMR students (1973). Most of the studies reviewed concern the educable mentally retarded (EMR). Lawrence and Winschel have pointed out that self-concept tests do not support segregation though evidence is inconclusive.

There is a lack of agreement about the influence of segregation versus non-segregation upon the self-concepts of EMR students. Do retarded children make realistic comparisons between their own achievements and those of non-retarded peers, and the comparisons, realistic or otherwise have a negative effect on their self-concepts? To what extent are retarded students aware of their status as "special class" segregated students?

Howe and Snider (1969) found out that EMR students of average IQ (71) and average age (14 years, 9 months), consistently over-rated themselves. It is suggested that for younger and duller students the over-rating would be larger. Ringness (1961) compared the self-concept of children of low, average and high intelligence and found that children of low intelligence overestimated their success. They were much less realistic about themselves than either the average or bright children. In all cases the self-estimates varied with sex and with the situation, as well as with intelligence. The self-ratings of the slower students were considerably less reliable.

McGarvie (1970) found that, within the EMR range, the higher the IQ, the higher the self-concept. He concluded that the EMR students were not oblivious of the behavior of others towards them.

Carroll (1967), investigating the self-concepts of EMR children discovered adverse effects of placement in special classes, since the EMR children felt the impact of being labelled as "below average." He

TABLE 1

1. I have lots of friends at my school	I have very few friends at my school	I have no good friends at my school
2. I usually do what I want to do	Sometimes I do what others want to do	Usually I do what others want to do
3. I am the smartest person in my own class	I am as smart as anyone in my own class	I am not as smart as most of those in my own class
4. I have lots of good ideas about how to do things	Sometimes I have good ideas about how to do things	I don't have any good ideas about how to do things
5. Most of the other students like me a lot	Some of the students like me	Hardly anyone at my school really likes me
6. I am pretty happy to be just the way I am	Sometimes I wish I were different from the way I am	I wish I could change lots of things about me
7. I talk to other students a lot	I sometimes talk to other students	I don't talk to other students very much
8. I like going to school	Sometimes I like going to school and sometimes I don't like to	I don't like going to school

found greater self-esteem among 9-year-old EMR students in partly integrated classes. Up to that time it was thought that children taken out of a regular school class and placed with others of similar ability would increase in self-esteem since they would be comparing themselves with others of similar ability instead of with students of much higher ability.

In contrast, Lewis (1972) found that the self-concept of EMR students in a segregated setting was higher than that of students in an integrated setting; segregated students compared themselves with their peers, not with a normal population. Students were not affected by being labelled as attending a "special" school. The longer the student is in the segregated setting the better his self-image. However, Lewis sees this as a negative effect since the self-image appears to be less realistic.

Mayer's findings that there was no difference in self-concepts of students related to the length of time they had spent in special classes support the opposite conclusion (1966). If placement in special classes is to be correlated with a lowering of self-esteem one would expect that there would be differences according to the length of time spent in such classes. Mayer's sample was much larger than that of Carroll.

The only study dealing with TMR students' self-concepts both within a semi-integrated and within a segregated setting is that of Hambleton and Ziegler (1972). Their technique relied upon the reports of regular school students of how they thought the retarded students felt about themselves. The technique is questionable if only upon the grounds that it would be very difficult for a child at the grade 5 or 6 level to make the kind of projection required. Indeed the projections themselves, such as the fact that the retarded children were more likely to see themselves as intelligent, may only be an expression of the myth of obliviousness cited by some earlier workers. There was no direct measure of the self-concept of the trainable mentally retarded students in Hambleton and Ziegler's investigation.

In almost the only direct study of self-concepts of trainable retarded students, in this case adults, Carr and McLaughlin (1973) found it was very difficult to assess self-concept of their students in an adult education class. Some difficulties probably account for the dearth of studies of self-concepts of TMR students.

Methodology

Subjects. There was a total of 60 students at the semi-integrated setting and 70 at the segregated setting. Subjects were selected for the self-concept test if they were able to communicate clearly enough to respond adequately to the interview. From those whose speech was clear, two matched groups were formed. There were 19 subjects at each setting, 12 of each group being male. Matching of the groups was in terms of age within 1½ years, IQ within 10 points, sex, and father's occupation. The average age for students was 16 years, 11 months at the semi-integrated setting and 16 years, 10 months at the segregated setting, with the average IQ at both settings being 45.1.

Interview Technique. A review of various tests of self-concept showed that standardized tests could not be used since there was none appropriate for the age and IQ range. It was also evident that the reading level within the tests was too high and that the length of time required for the student to attend was far too long.

Hambleton and Ziegler's technique of asking the regular school students about the self-concepts of the TMR students in their school was rejected on two counts. First, a preliminary questionnaire showed that few of the high school students could identify many of the TMR students. Second, it was desirable to compare self-concepts of students at semi-integrated and segregated settings. Since the investigator was a clinical psychologist experienced in interviewing retarded students an interview method of assessment of self-concept was possible with an in-process decision about the validity of the answers given.

The questions devised by Hambleton and Ziegler (1973) were at the appropriate cognitive level and sought the information needed. Each student was interviewed individually using these question topics.

Great care was taken not to lead the students to any particular response. Wherever there was any doubt in the interviewer's mind as to whether the student was expressing his own thoughts or simply saying what he thought was required, the questioning was continued until there was no reasonable doubt left as to the student's real attitude. All except two of the students were interviewed in English. The sample size was reduced to the final 19 at each setting when the results of one student at the semi-integrated setting and two at the segregated setting were discarded because the interviewer was not satisfied that a valid result had been obtained.

Results

Questions 2, 4 and 6 relate to general self-esteem, while the remaining questions measure school self-esteem. Following Richmond and Dalton (1973), the general self-esteem factor "attempts to assess the individual's perception of self apart from his interaction with others." From this definition, question 2 would be less a measure of general self-esteem than social self-esteem. However, it has been classed under general self-esteem since it carries little weight on its own as the third aspect of the self-concept. School self-esteem refers to "The child's perception of himself in the school setting."

The data were analyzed as follows:

Responses from the left hand column of the scales were scored 3; those in the middle column 2; and the right hand column 1. Analysis was for both general and school self-esteem.

The scores for each student and his "match" were analyzed by the sign test for two correlated samples.

For the general self concept, N (number of different signs) = 14; X (number of fewest signs) = 6; p = .791; for the school self-concept, N = 19; X = 7; p = .365. Thus, there was no difference between the self-concepts of TMR students in the two settings as measured by clinical interview technique.

Discussion

In the semi-integrated setting no special measures were taken to educate the high school students about the needs of TMR students. Semi-integration was undertaken to use available space. The school for the senior retarded students retained its separate identity and both schools moved into a new building together. There was little time or opportunity for attention to the process of semi-integration as both schools coped with the problems of moving.

Despite the absence of planning towards semi-integration, no significant differences were found between the self-concepts of students at this setting and those of students at the well-established segregated setting. These findings suggest that within the TMR range self-concepts are not adversely affected by placement in a regular high school. Since there was no difference between the self-concepts of stu-

dents in the segregated and semi-integrated settings, support is given neither to the notion that TMR students compare themselves adversely with normal students, nor to the idea that in a segregated setting they see themselves negatively as a result of attending a special school. The converse is also true since it may be interpreted that the self-concepts of both groups were equally poor. Perhaps the students at the semi-integrated setting compared themselves adversely to regular high school students, while the segregated ones felt badly about attending a school for the retarded. The latter argument was not supported by the clinical impressions of the interviewer. Overriding the secondary factors seemed to be the fact that both groups of students were happy with themselves in their own programs and did not think beyond their immediate environment.

References

Carr, C. C., & McLaughlin, J. A. Self-concepts of mentally retarded adults in an adult education class. *Mental Retardation*, 1973, **11**, 57–59.

Carroll, Anne Welch. The effects of segregated and partially integrated school programs on self-concept and academic achievements of educable mentally retarded. *Exceptional Children*, 1967, **34**, 93–99.

Foxcroft, R. *Teaching trainable retarded children: A new approach for Simcoe County*. (mimeographed) (Barrie, Ontario: Simcoe Board of Education, 1972.)

Hambleton, D,, & Ziegler, S. The Study of the integration of trainable retarded students into a regular elementary school setting. Toronto, 1973.

Howe, C. E., & Snider, B. Participation of retarded children in junior high academic and non-academic regular classes. *Exceptional Children*, 1969, **35**, 617–623.

Lawrence, Elizabeth A., & Winschel, James F. Self concept and the retarded: research and issues. *Exceptional Children*, 1973, **39**, 310–319.

Lewis, Tony. The self-concepts of adolescent educationally subnormal boys. *Educational Research*, 1972, **15**, 16–20.

Mayer, C. L. The relationships of early special class placement and the self-concepts of mentally handicapped children. *Exceptional Children*, 1966, **33**, 77–81.

McGarvie, D. J. The impact special education placement on the self-concept of adolescent educable mentally retarded students. Doctoral Dissertation, Marquette University, Ann Arbor, Michigan: University Microfilms, 1970, No. 71–5308.

Richmond, Bert O., & Dalton, J. Leon. Teacher ratings and self-concept reports of retarded pupils. *Exceptional Children*, 1973, **40**, 178–183.

Ringness, T. A. Self-concept of children of low, average, and high intelligence. *American Journal of Mental Deficiency*, 1961, **65**, 453–461.

Leisure Time Activities for Trainable Mentally Retarded Adolescents

ROBERT L. MARION

A s parents and teachers work together to help trainable mentally retarded adolescents reach their fullest potentials, the area of leisure time activities is often overlooked. Participation in leisure time activities is not only a concern of parents but also a source of stress for teachers of exceptional adolescents. Both teachers and parents voice frustration over the lack of simple inexpensive activities that can be easily contracted between teacher and parent and that can also be readily incorporated into the circle of family activities. Moreover, this frustration is magnified when teachers and parents attempt to plan leisure time activities for trainable mentally retarded adolescents.

The adolescent years of trainable mentally retarded (TMR) youths are often very trying for parents. Evidence of this was shown by the results of a questionnaire administered in 1976 by the author to parents of TMR adolescents in a Centex school district. The results revealed that for most of these adolescents (60%), watching television was the major leisure time activity. A 1974 study by Bernard Lax showed similar results. Lax found that 63% of the mentally retarded adolescents in his study spent the greater proportion of their time viewing television. The study also found that mothers tended to enjoy having the students at home immediately following graduation. However, as time progressed, they indicated that the adolescents got under foot and grew tired of watching television. Thus, sitting at home and watching television has remained the number one leisure time activity of TMR adolescents over extended time.

Parents and teachers need not despair, there are leisure time activities that lend themselves to adaptation with TMR adolescents. Within the concept of leisure time activities there are interactions that promote skill development through participation by TMR adolescents and their parents. Teachers can help parents find suitable activities in which to participate with their adolescent children.

GUIDELINES TO FOLLOW

When considering leisure time activities, parents and teachers should keep the following guidelines in mind:

1. Emphasis should be placed on *what* the youth is doing, not the end product.
2. Activities should be appealing and should be "fun" things to do.
3. Interest level of the parent about the activity should match that of the adolescent.
4. Relationship of the activity to previously learned tasks should be clear.
5. Uncleanliness involved in the activities should be within the parent's tolerance level and the youth's responsibility for cleanup.
6. Rules for the activities should be flexible.

These guidelines will allow parents and teachers to agree on activities for leisure time enjoyment. They will also guide parents and teachers in collaborative attempts for teaching specific skills in areas where TMR youths generally need assistance. The following activities can be easily included in a leisure time program for TMR adolescents and parents: gardening, hammering and nailing activities, and puppetry and plays. Gardening, hammering, nailing, and puppetry/play activities were selected as appropriate leisure time pursuits for several reasons. They can: (1) be readily engaged in by all parents, youths, and teachers; (2) be done with relatively small expense for all concerned parties; (3) lend themselves to teaching practices commonly applied to TMR's; (4) have carry over value to other life situations; and (5) be approached through scaled performance levels, i.e., simple to complex achievements.

In addition, three areas of skill development tend to fit the proposed leisure time activities: self concept, attention span, and socialization. The selection of self concept, attention span, and socialization as the three skill areas primarily evolved from two sources. First considerable research (Carlsen & Ginglend, 1968; Edmonson, 1970; Halpern, 1975) attested to the fact that TMR adolescents need help in further development of these skills. Second, additional evidence gathered through data collected by the author from summer camp participation and from therapeutic recreational activities involving adolescents supported the contention that these skills are in need of further development in TMR youths. Some of the activities could fit a separate category or all three of the areas. Parents should understand that this will not be unusual since every youth is different and has unique needs in this respect. Therefore, for ease of recognition, the activities are grouped under categorical listings, i.e., socialization, attention span, and self concept.

Although the categorical listings allow for ease of recognition, an important requirement in the planning of leisure programs is the choice of activities to bring about the desired skill development. General guidelines to follow are:

1. If teaching to develop socialization skills:
   a. Choose an activity that requires two or more people.
   b. Select activities that can be related to people and their jobs and/or functional living skills.
   c. Choose activities that have project capabilities and can foster cooperative efforts.
   d. Pick activities that promote family and sibling involvement.

2. If teaching to develop attention span skills:
   a. Determine activities that require sequential behavior patterns.

b. Choose activities that can be repeated if done poorly or incorrectly.

c. Select activities that develop specific abilities (coordination, dexterity).

3. If teaching for self concept skills:
   a. Choose activities that allow for positive reinforcement for good work or accomplishments.
   b. Select activities that can build decision making and problem solving skills.
   c. Pick activities that build confidence and self esteem.
   d. Select activities that develop good work habits (reliability, honesty).

Parents and teachers who work with TMR adolescents must also conceptualize the leisure time activities within the framework of the total educational plan. Some informal assessment is necessary to determine whether the desired outcomes are achieved to the satisfaction of parent, teacher, and the adolescent. A sample recording chart is offered as an informal guide for evaluating the progress of the child's ability to achieve satisfaction in the activity (see Figure 1). It also allows parents and teachers to measure the child's progress as he or she develops in self concept, attention span, and socialization skills.

**Indoor Calendar
Activity—Watering**

	Mon.	Tues.	Wed.	Thurs.	Fri.	Sat.	Sun.
Week 1							
Week 2							
Week 3							
Week 4							

Figure 1. A Sample Recording Chart.

GARDENING

Although this article confines itself to the explanation and monitoring of only one leisure time activity—gardening—two other proposed activities, hammering and nailing and puppetry and the attendant concepts of attention span and socialization, are included for parent and teacher consideration. All are inexpensive leisure time activities that can be readily adapted into the family circle.

Indoor Activities

Every day the youth remembers to water the plant without a weekly or daily reminder and parental assistance, a gold star can be placed in the appropriate space. A silver star can be used to indicate that parents had to remind the adolescent about the watering day or had to lend assistance in the watering chores. Finally, a blue star can be used to show that parents had to assume major responsibility for the task. By monitoring the task in this fashion, a student can move through the stages of parent initiated→ jointly initiated→ adolescent initiated activity. As a measure of growth in self concept, parents and youth can check the number of gold stars that appear on the chart.

Outdoor Activities

For outdoor activities (raking, watering, and weeding) the same star awarding system can be used to designate who initiates the activity. In addition, colored checks can be used to indicate the activities completed (blue check = raking, red check = watering, black check = weeding). Since the goal of the task is adolescent independence, the different colored checks serve to reinforce the idea that all tasks are to be completed satisfactorily. A gold star with three different colored check marks would indicate a perfect record. A youth might achieve various combinations of success en route. For instance, he or she might begin with a blue star accompanied by a red check and progress to a silver star with blue and black checks, and finally earn a gold star with three checks. By using this chart, parents and youths can measure the youth's progress by counting gold stars and the number of squares with three different colored check marks.

Self Concept

Activities that give adolescents a feeling of success, a product to show off, or confidence in themselves will improve their self concept. By planning a time for "show and tell," the family can give the youth an incentive to work toward. Family approval is usually necessary before an adolescent has the confidence to face peers.

The experience of planting and tending one's own plants either indoors or outdoors can give the youth a positive feeling. Whether the product is fruit, flowers, or just a green stalk, adolescents enjoy the watering and watching.

Plants can be obtained inexpensively from foods, as well as by purchasing seeds or small plants. The following types of foods will yield great house plants with little bother.

1. *Carrot* tops can be rooted in water and will produce a lot of leaves in a short time.
2. *Sweet potatoes* root and will grow for a long time in water. An old can will rust, but the added minerals will make the plants grow faster. They can also be placed in dirt after rooting. The only problem is to have enough room for all the vines that will grow!
3. *Lemon, orange,* and *grapefruit* seeds will sprout shiny green leaves. Grapefruit seeds are probably the easiest to sprout. Dry them out for a day or two before planting. They require a lot of water and like a great deal of sun.
4. *Avocado* pits make tall leafy plants. Dry out the pit for several days, then slit it all the way around lengthwise with a knife or razor blade. The pointed end should go up. Do not place the avocado pit all the way into the water or it will rot. It can be propped by toothpicks and rooted in water or placed immediately in dirt. The avocado roots slowly; sometimes it takes a month. They require a lot of water and sun for best results.
5. *Pineapple* tops make beautiful plants with sharp edged leaves. Cut the top off leaving approximately 1 inch of fruit. Let it dry out for several days. Remove the dried leaves and dried peel. You should now have a base below the green leaves of about 2 to 3 inches. This can be placed directly in dirt or in water to root. Pineapples require little water and alot of sun. This is a very easy plant to grow. It even likes old coffee grounds on its soil.
6. *Dried beans* will yield plants in a short period of time. However they will have to be moved outside and into large containers or the ground for best results.

Adolescents can work out a calendar for water schedules, using pictures on the days that need to be remembered. Overwatering is the adolescent's greatest mistake, causing plants to rot. If the plant belongs to the youth, he or she must learn from doing. If the youth is working in a gardening space outside, parents can give a boost to his or her feeling of pride if they allow the youth to have his or her own area of ground. The youth can then be held responsible for weeding, raking, and watering as needed. If the plants die, it must be as a result of the youth's actions and no one else's. If the garden is successful, the achievement belongs to the youth alone. Chances of success are fairly good, especially in sunny climates.

ATTENTION SPAN — HAMMERING AND NAILING

Adolescents may have the bodies of adults, but the habits of children. This is a common problem for everyone while growing up. Mentally handicapped adolescents generally develop at an even slower rate and their attention spans are shorter than expected for their age. Activities that build on shorter tasks will help increase these adolescents' attention span.

Most households have a hammer and a few nails. Lumber yards and construction sites will usually give parents a few pieces of scrap wood. The use of hammers and nails is not always associated with leisure time, but with work. Adolescents view tools as part of the adult world. Many decorative and useful items can be made with a piece of wood and some nails.

Parents can start the adolescent, who needs practice at staying with the task until completion, with a small project. After the youth has completed the initial task, he or she can then be moved to another simple task. As adolescents master the projects, they can attempt more complicated steps. Following are two sample activities and a list of the materials needed to carry them out.

Key Holder

One of the simplest things to make is a key holder. Materials needed include a piece of wood of any shape, three to six medium or large flat headed nails, and paint or stain (optional). If desired, the youth can begin by painting or staining the wood. Then, the nails can be hammered into the wood in a straight line or randomly. The youth can write or paint the word *keys* on the board and, with the help of his or her parents, the youth can label the nails for the various keys. Parents can add to the youth's sense of achievement by hanging the key holder in a visible place.

String Art

For a more advanced project, the youth can create a string design using the following materials: a piece of wood of any size or shape, a pen or felt tipped marker, medium sized nails with small heads, and colored yarn or string. Colored yarn or string can be purchased or white string can be dyed with food coloring. Again, the wood can be painted or stained before beginning the project.

To begin the project, the parent can draw dots on the board, forming a design. Then, the youth can hammer a nail on each dot. After the nailing is completed, the parents can show the youth how to criss-cross the string in order to form the design. Most arts and crafts stores have ready made designs and will help parents learn how to use the string.

For a more complex project, the youth can create his or her own design. The design can be drawn on paper at first, then transferred to the wood. The youth may then be ready to create a design directly on the wood. Any design is "good" if the artist likes it. Again, parents can add to the youth's sense of achievement by hanging the finished product on a wall.

SOCIALIZATION — PUPPETRY

Adolescents who are hindered by their level of intelligence frequently experience frustration when interacting with peers. Whenever possible, leisure activities including another participant should be structured for these children in order to encourage socialization. Board games, card games, and sports can be easily structured to emphasize group involvement.

Parents often overlook having adolescents instruct or entertain younger children. After playing and interacting with younger children, adolescents can gain the needed confidence to seek out peers. Puppet shows appeal to children of all ages. Adolescents can easily help younger children make the puppets and stage and put on a show.

Paper Bag Puppets

Paper bag puppets can be easily constructed using the following materials: paper bags of any size, construction paper, buttons, string or yarn, crayons, scraps of material, glue, and cotton balls. A face can be drawn on the fold side of the bag so that when one's hand is inside a mouth is created at the fold line. Eyes, noses, ears, hair, and clothing can be created from almost any available materials.

Sock Puppets

Sock puppets can be created using the following materials: old socks, thread and needle, buttons, sequins, and yarn. A face is all that needs to be created to make a sock into a puppet. If the youth does not know how to sew, items can be attached to the sock using a strong glue.

CONCLUSION

Leisure time activities can range from gardening to work related activities to pure entertainment. They can evolve into successful teaching/learning experiences for TMR adolescents and their parents. The leisure time activities described in this article have proved to be enjoyable, inexpensive, and adaptable to family situations. Parents, teachers, and adolescents all stand to gain by their participation in these activities. Teachers can work with parents to increase self concept, socialization, and attention span skills and development in adolescents. Parents will witness observable growth in their child's skill development through enjoyable leisure time activities. Finally, TMR youths will grow by participation in every day activities that promote leisure and learning.

REFERENCES

Carlsen, B., & Ginglend, D. *Recreation for retarded teenagers and young adults,* Nashville: Abingdon Press, 1968.

Edmonson, B. Social inference training of retarded adolescents. *Education and Training of the Mentally Retarded,* 1970, *15*(4), 169-176.

Halpern, A.S. Measuring social and prevocational awareness in mildly retarded adolescents. *American Journal of Mental Deficiency,* 1975, *80*(1), 81-89.

Establishing Play Behaviors in Mentally Retarded Youth

PAUL WEHMAN

Mr. Wehman is currently a doctoral student and research assistant in the Department of Studies in Behavioral Disabilities, University of Wisconsin-Madison. From 1972 to 1974 he was a psychologist at Lincoln State School, Lincoln, Ill. Prior to this he obtained an M.S. in psychology at Illinois State University. Mr. Wehman is a member of the Council for Exceptional Children and the American Association on Mental Deficiency. Requests for reprints of this article should be sent to: Paul Wehman, Department of Studies in Behavioral Disabilities, Waisman Center, University of Wisconsin, Madison, Wis. 53706.

THERE HAS BEEN a limited amount of experimental research reported on the various aspects of training mentally retarded youth in play skills. This is surprising in light of the generally held notion that play skill development enhances the likelihood of more advanced adaptive behavior, i.e., language and social skills (e.g., Piers[34]). Development of play behaviors in mentally retarded children and adolescents appears to be an area that behavior therapists have not extensively researched. Much of the reported behavioral play research has been carried out with normal preschool children.[17, 18, 35] Furthermore, play behaviors have rarely been used as a dependent variable. Usually play is manipulated as an independent variable with different indexes of social skills or intelligence measured.[30, 31, 49] The focus of the present paper is to look at play as a dependent variable. The rationale for this is: A mentally retarded population usually possesses few, if any, play behaviors. These behaviors must be taught before play can be used as a medium to facilitate socialization.

In a discussion of play it is difficult to make precise definitions. To define play explicitly is to defeat the inherent spontaneity and creativity that it is hoped will emerge in a free-play situation. Ellis[10] talks about play as,

. . . a process of experiencing exploration, investigation, and manipulation and it leads eventually to thinking involving the integration of previous with current experiences or epistemic behavior. *(p. 135)*

For the purpose of this paper, play is considered broadly as any set of activities in which the child engages over time and which, in effect, serve as functional reinforcers. The child should enjoy himself and have fun with these activities.[6] They should not be self-stimulatory, overly aggressive in nature, or disruptive. Obviously, this opens up a wide field of behaviors apart from traditional table games, blocks, puzzles, and so on. No specific limitations are made to the individual, as having to play in

"Establishing Play Behaviors in Mentally Retarded Youth," Paul Wehman, *Rehabilitation Literature*, Vol. 37, No. 8, August 1975. ©1975 by the National Easter Seal Society for Crippled Children and Adults, Chicago.

a group. It may be that certain children desire to play alone, and this is a choice behavior that should not be inhibited.

This paper presents an overview and discusses the evolution of different play theories and their respective validity. Experimental research relevant to the instructional aspects of teaching play to mentally retarded children is reviewed and evaluated. A three-stage interactive model is then presented as a viable framework for training mentally retarded students in play. Finally, some research directions and implications of play research are enumerated.

Overview of Theories of Play

The discussion on play theory is a selective review of the more predominant theories held to explain and predict play behavior. For an in-depth historical survey and comprehensive review of play theories, the reader is referred to Ellis.[10]

Psychoanalytic theory. Traditional approaches to explaining play behavior can be found in the related cathartic, psychoanalytic, and play therapy theories. Psychodynamic discussions of play typically view play as a means of satisfactory social outlet for frustration and aggression. The pleasure principle is another psychoanalytic construct used to account for the motivation to play. The player plays for the gratification that play brings. According to Erikson,[11] play is a vital process in establishing ego strength in children. Play therapy can be viewed as the change strategy that evolved out of the psychoanalytic formulations of play. Play therapy has been used with exceptional children as well as with normal children.[22] There is, unfortunately, insufficient experimental evidence with which to evaluate the tenability of psychodynamic-based play therapy as an effective change process.

Cognitive-developmental theory. The cognitive theory of Jean Piaget is another approach to studying play behavior. In Piagetian theory, play behaviors occur as a result of thought processes of the child interacting with environmental experiences. Children's play passes through developmental stages of increasingly sophisticated intellectual ability. Sequencing of cognitive development is more important than the variation in which children reach the different developmental milestones.

Flavell[13] reports how such an evolution of play occurs in the sensorimotor stage of Piaget's theory. Stage one is seen as "empty" behavior such as free sucking movements (without breast or bottle). Stage two demonstrates primary circular reactions such as a baby throwing its head back and laughing several times repetitively. Stage three finds that pure assimilation has developed in the form of means-ends behavior. For example, in this stage the child may act on the environmental object purely for the sake of the pleasure the object holds. In stage four the child begins to play more with the means rather than the ends. Stage five is characterized by the child acting in a more complex way on various stimuli in his field. Ritualization

begins to develop in this stage. Flavell[13] gives the following example of ritualization:

the child encounters some of the usual stimuli associated with going to sleep (e.g., pillow, blanket, etc.) and momentarily goes through the ritual of sleeping: he lies down, sucks his thumb, and so on. *(p. 128)*

Stage six finds the emergence of symbolization. The child now begins to show the ability to pretend or make believe.

Piaget[33] postulates that the sophistication of play behaviors evolves with increased cognitive complexity, which is derived from an expanding base of environmental experiences. The reader who desires a greater review of Piaget theory and play development is referred to Piaget.[33]

Learning theory. Play behaviors can also be explained in terms of learning theory, both operant conditioning and social learning.[12, 45] In an operant conditioning paradigm, play behaviors may develop in response to a variety of stimuli present in the environment. The response may be followed by positive external reinforcement or internal reinforcement, i.e., intrinsic enjoyment of exploration or manipulation of the environment. Play behaviors are strengthened with each subsequent response and reinforcement. Obviously, the operant conditioning paradigm places emphasis on environmental events and contingency arrangement as the influencing variables in the development of play behaviors.

Another aspect of learning theory that may account for patterns of play behaviors is social learning and imitation. A large body of research evidence currently exists to indicate that normal and retarded children acquire new behaviors through observational learning.[2, 29, 45] Recent research on play and social interaction skill development with severely retarded persons suggests that imitation learning may be a key factor in teaching methodology.[27, 47, 48] Sutton-Smith has proposed that child-rearing practices of different cultures are influential in the patterns of play behaviors that develop in children. For a complete discussion of the Sutton-Smith enculturation hypothesis, the reader is referred to Sutton-Smith and co-workers.[36, 37, 39, 40]

Arousal theory. A recent theory advanced by Ellis[10] to explain and predict play behavior is that of play as stimulus-seeking behavior. Ellis has done an excellent job of integrating information theory, behavior theory, and physiological psychology into a highly tenable theory of play. The basic thesis of arousal-seeking theory is that an organism requires stimulus diversity. Information flow is arousing and there is an optimal arousal level called *sensoristasis.* Sensoristasis is defined as

a drive state of cortical arousal which impels the organism (in a waking state) to strive to maintain an optimal level of sensory variation. There is, in other words, a drive to maintain cortical arousal at an optimal level.[38, p. 30]

Berlyne[5] discusses three stimulus properties, novelty, uncertainty, and complexity, which all may reflect environmental diversity. These can be seen as key variables for play behaviors to develop, particularly in the mentally retarded child who may have serious attending behavior deficits. Ellis states that intermediate novelty of a stimulus is preferred; complete or absolute novelty may be aversive or there may be no past reference with which the individual can compare. Uncertainty refers to varying the outcomes expected so that total predictability is not possible by the organism. Complexity of a stimulus event is achieved by,

> . . . increasing the number of distinguishable components, by increasing the dissimilarity of the components, and by manipulating the elements so that they cannot be categorized as just one item reacted to simply.[10, p. 92]

The arousal-seeking behavior theory of play lends itself to isolating some of the components necessary in helping retarded children acquire play behaviors. Some of the issues this theory raises may be most helpful in devising appropriate play materials as well. This area is discussed in greater depth later in the article.

Development of Play Behaviors—
A Review of the Research

The basic theme of the present paper deals with how to build play skills into the behavioral repertoire of mentally retarded youth. The ease with which play responses are acquired varies with the ability level of the individual, i.e., present behavioral repertoire, the complexity of the play skill, and the efficacy of the teaching procedure. Unfortunately, there is a paucity of empirical evidence dealing with these salient variables and their interrelationships.

Early research by Mehlman[26] focused attention on the effects group play therapy has on personality and intelligence of mildly retarded children. It was found that statistically significant changes were measured in personality but not in intelligence. No explicit descriptions of the play therapy process were given. Personality was measured by the California Test and Rorschach testing and intelligence was assessed through the Stanford-Binet and Grace Arthur Test. In another report, a demonstration project of play therapy for institutionalized retarded children was described.[4] It was noted that mentally retarded children play less because of a prevalent attitude seen in ward aides and many professionals—that mentally retarded people cannot be taught to play. Furthermore, the design of play materials is not appropriate for the mentally retarded. By the time many retarded children have developed intellectually to the point of playing with certain materials, they are physically too big for them or frequently break the materials. Benoit[4] states,

> To begin with the more obvious they learn very slowly, require much repetition, depend on examples more than words, attend to things rather than to ideas; as a result of these and related traits, they have much difficulty in handling numbers and words, and hence are not likely to be good at or fond of reading, writing, and arithmetic. (p. 44)

Research by Leland, Walker, and Taboada[23] revealed that group play therapy with moderately retarded boys increased scores on the Vineland Social Quotient and Wechsler Intelligence Test (WISC). No specific teaching procedures or descriptions of the methods employed were given, although it was found that the children were more responsive when the therapist was directive during play time.

In a more extensive study by Newcomer and Morrison,[30] the effects of group versus individual play therapy were compared on four scales with 12 mild to moderately retarded institutionalized children. The Denver Developmental Screening Test was adapted for use as a pretest–post-test measure of development. The four categories of abilities included gross motor skills, fine motor skills, language skills, and social skills. Play therapy involved a broad spectrum of activities such as playing with blocks, wagons, push-pull toys, pegboards, scissors, puzzles, naming body parts, imitating speech sounds, self-feeding, dressing (buttons and zippers), and talking on a telephone. The group play or individual play subjects first received sessions of directive therapy, then nondirective, and last directive therapy. A control group received no play therapy. Results indicated the following:

- All children receiving play therapy showed statistically significant gains across the four developmental categories measured.
- No clear-cut differences in developmental gains emerged as a result of individual versus group play therapy manipulations.
- Anecdotally, it was observed that a directive teaching style was more influential in helping achieve developmental gains than a nondirective style.

A major difficulty with the Newcomer and Morrison study[30] is that it does not lend itself to replicability. There is no clear-cut description of the procedures used to invoke the developmental gains other than the active or passive role played by the therapist. Furthermore, with such a broad array of materials and skills used to make up play therapy, it becomes difficult to identify the components of the process instrumental in facilitating the behavioral change of the children.

In a follow-up study, also using the Denver Developmental Screening Test as the criterion measure, Morrison and Newcomer[28] compared directive with nondirective play therapy procedures with mildly retarded institutionalized children. No statistically significant effects were noted, although there were significant differences between both groups and a control group on the Personal-Social and Fine-Motor Scales. These results shed little light on teaching methodology but do lend some credence to play as a medium of behavior development. One drawback to the results, however, is the failure to report reliability of behavior observation on the Denver Developmental Screening Test.

Recently, there has been an increasing interest in programing play skills with severely retarded children. One study by Whitman and others looked at the effects simple play behaviors have on social interactions.[49] A ball-rolling task and block-passing task were shaped in two severely retarded children, using positive reinforcement. Social responses were defined as "one child's behavior becoming mutually or reciprocally involved with a second child's behavior." Generalization of interactions was established across two peers other than the original subjects. An ABA reversal design was utilized and demonstrated the functional effects that the reinforcement contingency had on the average minutes of social interaction.

In another report, Kazdin and Erickson[21] extended the results of Whitman and coworkers with a larger subject base of 15 severely and profoundly institutionalized retarded adolescents. Shaping procedures were similar, but compliance with verbal instructions ("roll the ball" and "catch the ball") was measured as the dependent variable rather than the play responses. A multiple base line design across four subgroups of the subject population was employed to verify the experimental effect of the reinforcement contingency. One finding of particular significance in this study was that groups of subjects who had increasingly longer pretreatment base lines (e.g., received treatment later in the multiple base line design) showed increasing compliance with instructions during the base line. Kazdin and Erickson[21] speculate that this may have occurred as a function of repeated instructions and modeling (observation of a peer who complied with instructions). This finding may be indicative of the effects peer modeling has on the play behavior of the retarded.

Morris and Dolker[27] specifically examined the effects of a higher functioning peer model on the cooperative play of a severely retarded child. Results indicated that the low-interacting child displayed the most cooperative play under conditions of a shaping procedure and playing with a peer model. Ball-rolling was considered as play behavior in this study also.

One of the few attempts to evaluate objectively play behaviors of severely retarded children on a social interaction scale was completed by Paloutzian and his colleagues.[31] Imitation, prompting, and reinforcement were used to develop cooperative play behaviors, utilizing an adapted scale that arranged into a hierarchy play categories of autistic, unoccupied, independent, observing, attempted interaction, parallel, associative, and cooperative. Cooperative play was defined as passing a bean bag, pushing another child in a swing, pulling a peer in a wagon, or rocking a peer on a toy horse. The dependent variable measured was the change in scale score from pretest to post-test. Twenty subjects were divided equally into an experimental group and a control group. Results indicated that the experimental group showed a statistically significant increase in scores from pretest to post-test. Also, it was found that the social interaction skills acquired during training generalized to other environments.

Only two play programs were found that employed a task analysis teaching method.[3, 32] Eight children of varying degrees of retardation (mild to severe) were trained to pedal a tricycle independently.[32] Pedaling rotations and sessions, to criterion, were measured and food, social- and rest-play reinforcers were used as the independent variable. Fixed-interval and fixed-ratio reinforcement schedules were used to establish behavior maintenance. In another program conducted at a large state institution for the mentally retarded, four severely retarded adolescents were trained to play a table game, Candyland, using a step-by-step task analysis approach.[3] Greater cooperative play and spontaneity in other social behaviors were observed anecdotally as outcomes of this program.

Recently, the author completed two research studies aimed at increasing actions on a wide range of play materials and toys in withdrawn severely retarded adults[48] and at developing cooperative peer interactions between workshop clients during a leisure-time play period.[47] Both programs were evaluated in an across-subject, multiple base line design with a social reinforcement contingency placed on appropriate play behavior and social interactions. In both reports it was noted that subjects displayed a high frequency of self-stimulatory rocking behaviors initially. Through the social reinforcement intervention, these inappropriate social behaviors decreased to a low level, while play and social behaviors increased substantially. These studies represent one of the first systematic attempts at developing play behaviors across a wide range of play materials in a severely retarded population.

In a related report,[19] four profoundly retarded children were taught appropriate play behaviors in a classroom situation. The principal dependent variable was also percent of appropriate interaction with play objects. However, in this program the adult trainers were systematically removed (faded) from the teaching situation. Initially, there were three trainers, then two trainers, and finally one. At the completion of the program, no trainers were present in the play area and the children still continued to play independently at a rate higher than in the pretreatment period. This is significant, as it appears to be one of the few reports that demonstrate transfer of stimulus control from teacher training cues to the reinforcing properties of the play materials. Unfortunately, this program was not conducted in a rigorous experimental design and, hence, experimental verification of the teaching contingency is not possible.

In reviewing the present experimental evidence, it is apparent that there has been little coordinated and purposeful integration of play research. No research strategy of studying play behavior of the retarded has emerged as evidenced by the incongruent measures of play in the studies reviewed. Three of the studies consider rolling a ball as development of "play." Surprisingly, only one report was found that demonstrated acquisition of a table game skill. In several reports where play was manipulated as the independent variable and social behavior, or IQ as a change measure, no specific descriptions of the teaching procedures were provided. Furthermore, in those studies that directly measured play behavior, combinations of physical prompting, imitation, and reinforcement were used as the independent variable, thus confounding specific experimental effects. Researchers have not systematically expanded the play skill repertoire of retarded children and adolescents and have been too isolated in their focus. Finally, no clear-cut empirical evidence has been advanced to support training of play skills in retarded youth as an intensive programming technique that might foster advances in overall adaptive behavior.

A Model for Programing Play Skills to Mentally Retarded Youth

There appear to be interacting variables that should be considered in the development of play behaviors in mentally retarded youth. These variables are: current behavioral capabilities of the individual; efficacy of the teaching procedure being utilized to build the play behaviors; and horizontal range and vertical hierarchy of the play skills presented.

The following discussion examines these variables, their interrelationships, and how they can be conceptualized into a model (*see* the figure). The model presented is descriptive only and crude in nature. The purpose of the model is to serve as an initial attempt to identify and integrate some of the various components in the process of play development.

Initially, the mentally retarded student should be thoroughly evaluated to determine his present behavioral capacities. A physical examination to determine the extent of any motor or sensory handicap should be completed. Then, a full review of his behavioral repertoire must be carried out. This includes an analysis of imitation behaviors, tracking and searching skills, language competencies, and social interaction skills. Currie[9] has presented an excellent framework for which a behavioral evaluation can be initiated. It is expected that the repertoire of play behaviors as well as other behaviors should be constantly accumulating with proper teaching methods and environmental stimulation. Thorough client evaluation is a necessity that leads to correct selection of the appropriate operant level to begin training.

The writer has suggested a behavioral approach to assessing the play of mentally handicapped children in a clinical setting.[43] Several behavioral variables have rarely been measured and examined by researchers and clinicians.

These include: frequency of action on play materials and toys; diversity of play behaviors, i.e., frequency of novel responses; range of toys or materials acted on; frequency of interaction between peers and number of different peers interacted with; affective or aggressive behavior during play periods.

A greater emphasis on scrutinizing overt play behaviors

is advocated, rather than drawing often faulty inferences from psychodynamic aspects of children's play.

The "how" of training the mentally retarded in play skills remains an area where much research is required, although it is probably safe to say that imitation and modeling[12, 45] have a significant role. Presently, no definitive or precise teaching procedures have been reported in developing play skills. This deficit becomes particularly salient in trying to teach play skills to the more severely retarded child. A major reason for this deficit may be that free play behaviors should be creative and spontaneous. Development of creativity is difficult enough with normal children.[25] With severely handicapped students who frequently lack functional language and attending skills, teaching spontaneous play becomes most problematical.

A partial solution to this problem could lie in broadly defining the parameters of play behaviors. It may be more appropriate for students to act on a wide range of parallel activities at a low developmental level, rather than achieving extreme sophistication in one play skill, i.e., block design. A realistic goal might then be to make a wide spectrum of play materials eventually serve as different discriminative stimuli (signals) for the children's play behaviors. Of course, this would require careful planning of stimulus transfer by the teacher. Research needs to be done to determine the optimal presentation of play materials for maximizing a full range of play responses. While a task analysis approach has been used successfully in teaching mentally retarded students,[7] it may not be the most effective way of teaching play. Perhaps, a larger number of different play materials should be presented to students and only basic play skills be modeled, i.e., rolling clay into a ball, stacking blocks upward. From these basic models the student would act "freely" or "creatively" and be subsequently reinforced by the teacher for appropriate responses within the defined parameters. While this solution might lend itself to a greater array and diversity or response spontaneity, it also presents complications of lack of preciseness and basic problems in discrete response measurement. For example, if behavior change (increase in play skills) does occur, can we say it is a function of the *teaching method,* or just that the teacher happened to be a very good behavior shaper? For results of a play program to be replicable, teaching procedures must be clearly outlined and delineated.

A brief word should be mentioned about the method and style of positive reinforcement delivered. While this to some extent varies as a function of the severity of retardation, some general rules of reinforcement should be kept in mind during play periods:

1. Social reinforcement should be most expressive and explicit in what play behavior is being reinforced.
2. Reinforcement must occur contingently and immediately as an appropriate play skill unfolds; during play periods a series of play skills may develop rapidly and hence go unreinforced.
3. Social reinforcement must be faded to the intrinsic

An Interactive Model for Training
Play Skills in Mentally Retarded Youth

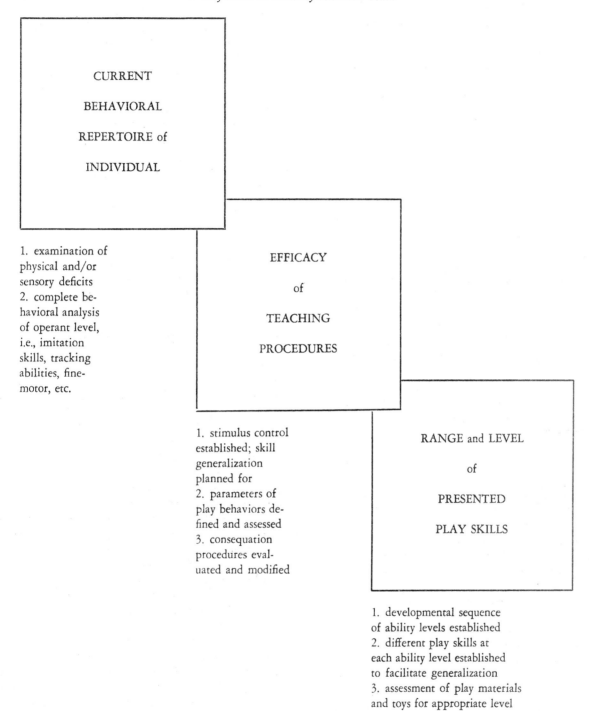

CURRENT

BEHAVIORAL

REPERTOIRE of

INDIVIDUAL

1. examination of
physical and/or
sensory deficits
2. complete be-
havioral analysis
of operant level,
i.e., imitation
skills, tracking
abilities, fine-
motor, etc.

EFFICACY

of

TEACHING

PROCEDURES

1. stimulus control
established; skill
generalization
planned for
2. parameters of
play behaviors de-
fined and assessed
3. consequation
procedures eval-
uated and modified

RANGE and LEVEL

of

PRESENTED

PLAY SKILLS

1. developmental sequence
of ability levels established
2. different play skills at
each ability level established
to facilitate generalization
3. assessment of play materials
and toys for appropriate level

reinforcement of engaging in playful behaviors; ul-
timately this will be a primary factor in maintaining
the play behavior.

Generalization of play behaviors is another component
of play development that must be programed to insure that
play skills will occur in many environments. Gardner[16]

makes several suggestions that are highly pertinent to a
discussion of play skill generalization. Some of the helpful
hints Gardner gives are:

1. Increase the similarity between the training setting and
other settings in which the behavior is expected to
occur.

2. Practice the new behavior in numerous settings.
3. Train people in the natural environments in which the child lives to use discriminative and reinforcing events in a manner similar to the training procedures.
4. Teach the child to manage his own behavior. (p. 121-123)

This suggests that effective parent training in behavior management techniques would be most helpful in facilitating transfer of play skills to different environments. Perhaps the most important hint Gardner gives is in point 4, that of teaching the child appropriate self-control methods. If retarded children can acquire the ability to cue themselves to act appropriately on play materials and sustain play behaviors by self-reinforcement, generalization, and transfer of training, problems will diminish.

A need exists to establish a play skill curriculum for mentally retarded children. A broad range of play skills arranged horizontally in conjunction with a logically sequenced ability hierarchy is needed for programing direction for the student. Potentially fruitful sources for beginning the development of such a curriculum might come from the work done by Florey,[14] Zimmerman and Calovini,[50] and the earlier mentioned study by Currie.[9] These authors suggest appropriate play materials and activities for different early childhood levels and present viable play development classification schemes. Such a curriculum should include general ability levels arranged in a hierarchical fashion and according to milestones that might correspond to Piagetian-type developmental stages, i.e., sensorimotor, preoperational. Response generalization at each ability level would be facilitated through horizontal programing of many different play skills across respective ability levels. With successful acquisition of new play responses, the student would have a foundation from which to develop choice behaviors. Only empirical data could eventually establish the validity of such a curriculum.

The writer has made an initial attempt toward the organization of a leisure-time activities curriculum for developmentally disabled persons.[46] A five-tiered arrangement of leisure-time activities is advanced and includes:

  I. Action on Play Materials;
  II. Passive Leisure;
  III. Game Activities;
  IV. Hobby Activity; and
  V. Active Socialization.

Each tier is subdivided into several leisure-time behaviors of progressive difficulty. Empirical research is required to substantiate the hierarchical sequencing of activities and to investigate optimal training methods for different components of the curriculum.

Future Research Directions

It is evident from the research review that there is minimal systematic experimental research or working models in the area of play development of mentally retarded youth. There are a number of research questions remaining to be answered.

An issue most germane to a discussion of play and mentally retarded students is: Precisely what are the effects of play skills on overall adaptive behavior? The effects of play development on sensorimotor skills, social behavior, and language remain largely an empirical question yet to be answered.

Also, the role of play materials and toys in the play behavior of retarded youth remains unclear and requires investigation. Ellis[10] presents some criteria that might serve as rough guidelines for play material selection:

1. Children play for the stimulation they receive;
2. that stimulation must contain elements of uncertainty (they are to some extent novel, complex, or dissonant); and
3. the interactions producing the stimulation must rise in complexity with the accumulation of knowledge about or experience with the object. (p. 135)

In several studies with normal infants, McCall[24] found that configural complexity, sound potential, and plasticity were critical stimulus properties in developing playful behaviors. Research on toy preference is required to evaluate the influence of these stimulus characteristics on the play of retarded students. Quilitch and Risley[35] have provided evidence that different play materials have differential effects on social play with preschool children. These authors found that certain games and materials (Pick up Stix, checkers) lend themselves to cooperative play, where other materials (Tinker Toys, clay) influenced greater frequency of isolate play behaviors. Other research also suggests the influential effects that play materials can have on play behaviors.[8, 20, 42]

Another unclear area in play program development is the problem of reinforcement and stimulus control. It is vital that external teacher reinforcement be faded to the intrinsically reinforcing properties that playful behaviors should possess. Furthermore, it is important that play materials become discriminative stimuli for play behaviors rather than teacher priming and cueing. It would be most helpful to answer two questions in this area of transfer of stimulus control: 1. Can play materials acquire stimulus control properties from teacher cueing? 2. If so, what are the optimal methods for enhancing stimulus transfer from teacher cues to play materials?

Without appropriate stimulus and reinforcement control, students will not maintain play behaviors. Systematic research is also needed to ascertain whether play behaviors fall into an individual response class, such as imitation behaviors.[1] It may be that different response classes of play behaviors are present at different hierarchical levels of intellectual development. Research needs to be done to determine whether playful behaviors such as exploring and manipulating the environment are generalized responses. This could possibly make up one horizontal programing level and have serious implications for the training methods utilized.

Finally, it is fervently hoped that some empirical evidence begins to accumulate in support of one theoretical position in play skill development. There is a critical need to give teachers of exceptional children program guidelines for training play behaviors. With the increasing sophistication of behavior technology in such complex areas as language development[15] and self-control,[41, 44] achieving play skill development in retarded youth is certainly within the grasp of behavior therapists.

List of References

1. Baer, Donald M.; Peterson, Robert F.; and Sherman, James A. The Development of Imitation by Reinforcing Behavioral Similarity to a Model. *J. Exper. Analysis of Behavior.* Sept., 1967. 10:5:405-416.

2. Bandura, Albert. *Principles of Behavior Modification.* New York: Holt, Rinehart, and Winston, 1969.

3. Bates, P., and Harrison, C. Teaching Severely Retarded Adolescents to Play Candyland. Unpublished paper, Lincoln State School, Lincoln, Ill., 1975.

4. Benoit, E. Paul. The Play Problem of Retarded Children: A Frank Discussion with Parents. *Am. J. Mental Deficiency.* July, 1955. 60:1:41-55.

5. Berlyne, D. E. *Conflict, Arousal, and Curiosity.* New York: McGraw-Hill, 1960.

6. Berlyne, D. E. Laughter, Humor, and Play, p. 795-852, in: Lindzey, Gardner L., and Aronson, Elliot, *eds. Handbook of Social Psychology. Vol. 3.* Reading, Mass.: Addison-Wesley, 1969.

7. Brown, Lou. Instructional Programs for Trainable-Level Retarded Students, in: Mann, Lester, and Sabatino, David A., *eds. The First Review of Special Education. Vol. 2.* Philadelphia (3515 Woodhaven Rd.): JSE Pr., 1973.

8. Buell, Joan, and others. Collateral Social Development Accompanying Reinforcement of Outdoor Play in a Preschool Child. *J. Applied Behavior Analysis.* 1968. 1:2:167-173.

9. Currie, Catherine. Evaluating Function of Mentally Retarded Children Through the Use of Toys and Play Activities. *Am. J. Occupational Ther.* Jan.-Feb., 1969. 23:1:35-42.

10. Ellis, M. J. *Why People Play.* Englewood Cliffs, N.J.: Prentice-Hall, 1973.

11. Erikson, Erik H. *Childhood and Society.* New York: Norton, 1950.

12. Fechter, John V., Jr. Modeling and Environmental Generalization by Mentally Retarded Subjects of Televised Aggressive or Friendly Behavior. *Am. J. Mental Deficiency.* Sept., 1971. 76:2:266-267.

13. Flavell, John H. *The Developmental Psychology of Jean Piaget.* Princeton, N.J.: D. Van Nostrand, 1963.

14. Florey, Linda. An Approach to Play and Play Development. *Am. J. Occupational Ther.* Sept., 1971. 25:6:275-280.

15. Garcia, Eugene E., and DeHaven, Everett D. Use of Operant Techniques in the Establishment and Generalization of Language: A Review and Analysis. *Am. J. Mental Deficiency.* Sept., 1974. 79:2:169-178.

16. Gardner, William I. *Children with Learning and Behavior Problems: A Behavior Management Approach.* Boston: Allyn and Bacon, 1974.

17. Goetz, Elizabeth M., and Baer, Donald M. Social Control of Form Diversity and the Emergence of New Forms in Children's Blockbuilding. *J. Applied Behavior Analysis.* Summer, 1973. 6:2:209-217.

18. Hart, Betty M., and others. Effect of Contingent and Non-Contingent Social Reinforcement on the Cooperative Play of a Preschool Child. *J. Applied Behavior Analysis.* 1968. 1:1:73-76.

19. Hopper, C. Toward the Development of Assessment and Remediation Procedures for the Play Skills of Young Severely Handicapped Students. Unpublished Master's Thesis, Department of Studies in Behavior Disabilities, University of Wisconsin, Madison, 1975.

20. Hulson, E. L. An Analysis of the Free Play of Ten Four-Year-Old Children Through Consecutive Observations. *J. Juvenile Research.* 1930. 14:188-208.

21. Kazdin, A., and Erickson, B. Developing Responsiveness to Instructions in Severely and Profoundly Retarded Residents. *J. Behavior Ther. and Experimental Psychiat.* In press.

22. Klein, Melanie. The Psychoanalytic Play Technique. *Am. J. Orthopsychiat.* Apr., 1955. 25:2:223-237.

23. Leland, Henry; Walker, John; and Taboada, Adoniram Nieves. Group Play Therapy with a Group of Post-Nursery Male Retardates. *Am. J. Mental Deficiency.* Mar., 1959. 63:5:848-851.

24. McCall, R. Exploratory Manipulation and Play in the Human Infant. *Monograph of the Society for Research in Child Development.* Chicago: Univ. of Chicago Pr., 1974.

25. Maltzman, Irving. On the Training of Originality. *Psychological Rev.* July, 1960. 67:4:229-242.

26. Mehlman, Benjamin. Group Play Therapy with Mentally Retarded Children. *J. Abnormal and Social Psychol.* Jan., 1953. 48:1:53-60.

27. Morris, Richard J., and Dolker, Michael. Developing Cooperative Play in Socially Withdrawn Retarded Children. *Mental Retardation.* Dec., 1974. 12:6:24-27.

28. Morrison, Thomas L., and Newcomer, Barbara L. Effects of Directive vs. Nondirective Play Therapy with Institutionalized Retarded Children. *Am. J. Mental Deficiency.* May, 1975. 79:2:666-669.

29. Nelson, Rosemery; Gibson, Frank, Jr.; and Cutting, D. Scott. Video Taped Modeling: The Development of Three Appropriate Social Responses in a Mildly Retarded Child. *Mental Retardation.* Dec., 1973. 11:6:24-27.

30. Newcomer, Barbara L., and Morrison, Thomas L. Play Therapy with Institutionalized Mentally Retarded Children. *Am. J. Mental Deficiency.* May, 1974. 78:6:727-733.

31. Paloutzian, Raymond F., and others. Promotion of Positive Social Interaction in Severely Retarded Children. *Am. J. Mental Deficiency.* Jan., 1971. 75:4:519-524.

32. Peterson, Rolf A., and McIntosh, Eranell I. Teaching Tricycle Riding. *Mental Retardation.* Oct., 1973. 11:5:32-34.

33. Piaget, Jean. *Play, Dreams and Imitation in Childhood.* (Trans. by C. Gattegno and F. M. Hodgson) New York: Norton, 1962. London: Routledge and Kegan Paul, 1951, reissued, 1962.

34. Piers, Maria W., *ed. Play and Development: A Symposium.* New York: Norton, 1972.

35. Quilitch, H. Robert, and Risley, Todd R. The Effects of Play Materials on Social Play. *J. Applied Behavior Analysis.* Winter, 1973. 6:4:573-578.

36. Roberts, John M., and Sutton-Smith, Brian. Child Training and Game Involvement. *Ethnology*. 1962. 1:166-185.

37. Roberts, John M.; Sutton-Smith, Brian; and Kendon, Adam. Strategy in Games and Folk-Tales. *J. Social Psychol.* 1963. 61:2:185-199.

38. Schultz, Duane P. *Sensory Restriction: Effects on Behavior*. New York: Academic Pr., 1965.

39. Sutton-Smith, Brian. The Meeting of Maori and European Cultures and Its Effect upon the Unorganized Games of Maori Children. *J. Polynesian Society*. 1951. 60:93-107.

40. Sutton-Smith, Brian. Play Preference and Play Behavior: A Validity Study. *Psychological Reports*. Feb., 1965. 16:1:65-66.

41. Thoresen, Carl Edwin, and Mahoney, Michael J. *Behavioral Self-Control*. New York: Holt, Rinehart, and Winston, 1974.

42. Van Alstyne, Dorothy. *Play Behavior and Choice of Play Materials in Pre-School Children*. Chicago: Univ. of Chicago Pr., 1932.

43. Wehman, Paul. A Behavioral Approach to Assessing the Play of Mentally Retarded Children. Unpublished manuscript, Univ. of Wis., Madison, 1975.

44. Wehman, Paul. Behavioral Self-Control with the Mentally Retarded. *J. Applied Rehab. Counseling*. Spring, 1975. 6:1:27-34.

45. Wehman, Paul. Imitation as a Facilitator of Treatment for the Mentally Handicapped. *Rehab. Lit*. In press.

46. Wehman, Paul. A Leisure Time Activities Curriculum for the Developmentally Disabled. *Journal of Developmental Disabilities*. In press.

47. Wehman, Paul, and Rettie, C. Cooperative Social Interactions Between Severely Retarded Workshop Clients During Leisure Time. Submitted for publication.

48. Wehman, Paul, and Rettie, C. Increasing Actions on Play Materials by Severely Retarded Women Through Social Reinforcement. Submitted for publication.

49. Whitman, Thomas L.; Mercurio, J. R.; and Caponigri, Vicki. Development of Social Responses in Two Severely Retarded Children. *J. Applied Behavior Analysis*. Summer, 1970. 3:2:133-138.

50. Zimmerman, Lyndall D., and Calovini, Gloria. Toys As Learning Materials for Preschool Children. *Exceptional Children*. May, 1971. 37:9:642-654.

FOCUS...

Developmental Characteristics of Mentally Retarded Persons

Degrees of Mental Retardation	Pre-School Age 0-5 Maturation and Development	School Age 6-20 Training and Education	Adult 21 and Over Social and Vocational Adequacy
Mild	Can develop social and communication skills; minimal retardation in sensorimotor areas; often not distinguished from normal until later age.	Can learn academic skills up to approximately sixth grade level by late teens. Can be guided toward social conformity. "Educable"	Can usually achieve social and vocational skills adequate to minimum self-support but may need guidance and assistance when under unusual social or economic stress.
Moderate	Can talk or learn to communicate; poor social awareness; fair motor development; profits from training in self-help; can be managed with moderate supervision.	Can profit from training in social and occupational skills; unlikely to progress beyond second grade level in academic subjects; may learn to travel alone in familiar places.	May achieve self-maintenance in unskilled or semi-skilled work under sheltered conditions; needs supervision and guidance when under mild social or economic stress.
Severe	Poor motor development; speech is minimal; generally unable to profit from training in self-help; little or no communication skills.	Can talk or learn to communicate; can be trained in elemental health habits; profits from systematic habit training	May contribute partially to self-maintenance under complete supervision; can develop self-protection skills to a minimal useful level in controlled environment.
Profound	Gross retardation; minimal capacity for functioning in sensorimotor areas; needs nursing care.	Some motor development present; may respond to minimal or limited training in self-help.	Some motor and speech development; may achieve very limited self-care; needs nursing care.

Appendix: Agencies and Services for Exceptional Children

Alexander Graham Bell Association for the Deaf
3417 Volta Place, N.W.
Washington, D.C. 20007

Allergy Foundation of America
801 Second Avenue
New York, New York 10017

American Academy for Cerebral Palsy
1255 New Hampshire Avenue, N.W.
Washington, D.C. 20036

American Academy of Child Psychiatry
1800 R Street, N.W.
Washington, D.C. 20009

American Academy of Pediatrics
1801 Hinman Avenue
Evanston, Illinois 60204

American Alliance for Health, Physical Education
and Recreation
1201 16th Street, N.W.
Washington, D.C. 20036

American Association for the Education of the
Severely and Profoundly Handicapped
P.O. Box 15287
Seattle, Washington 98115

American Association for Gifted Children
15 Gramercy Park
New York, New York 10003

American Association of Psychiatric Services
for Children
250 West 57th Street
New York, New York 10019

American Association of Special Educators
107-20 125th Street
Richmond Hill, New York 11419

American Association of Workers for the Blind, Inc.
Suite 637
1151 K Street, N.W.
Washington, D.C. 20005

American Association of University Affiliated
Programs for the Developmentally Disabled
1100 17th Street, N.W.
Washington, D.C. 20036

American Association on Mental Deficiency
5201 Connecticut Avenue, N.W.
Washington, D.C. 20015

American Bar Association
Commission on the Mentally Disabled
1800 M Street, N.W.
Washington, D.C. 20036

American Civil Liberties Union
85 Fifth Avenue
New York, New York 10011

American Coalition for Citizens with Disabilities
1346 Connecticut Avenue, N.W.
Washington, D.C. 20036

American Diabetes Association
18 E. 48th Street
New York, New York 10017

American Foundation for the Blind
15 West 16th Street
New York, New York 10011

American Genetic Association
1028 Connecticut Avenue, N.W.
Washington, D.C. 20036

American Medical Association
535 North Dearborn Street
Chicago, Illinois 60610

American Occupational Therapy Foundation
6000 Executive Boulevard
Rockville, Maryland 20852

American Physical Therapy Association
1156 15th Street, N.W.
Washington, D.C. 20005

American Psychological Association
1200 17th Street, N.W.
Washington, D.C. 20036

American Psychiatric Association
1700 18th Street, N.W.
Washington, D.C. 20009

American Schizophrenia Association
Huxley Institute
1114 First Avenue
New York, New York 10021

American Speech and Hearing Association
9030 Old Georgetown Road
Bethesda, Maryland 20014

Arthritis Foundation
1212 Avenue of the Americas
New York, New York 10036

Association for the Aid of Crippled Children
345 E. 46th Street
New York, New York 10017

Association for Children with Learning Disabilities
5225 Grace Street
Pittsburgh, Pennsylvania 15236

Association for Education of the Visually
Handicapped
1604 Spruce Street
Philadelphia, Pennsylvania 19103

Bureau of the Education of the Handicapped
400 Maryland Avenue, S.W.
Washington, D.C. 20202

Center for Law and Social Policy
1751 N Street, N.W.
Washington, D.C. 2009

Child Study Center
Yale University
333 Cedar Street
New Haven, Connecticut 06520

Child Welfare League of America
67 Irving Place
New York, New York 10003

Children's Bureau
Administration for Children, Youth and Families
P.O. Box 1182
Washington, D.C. 20013

Children's Defense Fund
1763 R Street, N.W.
Washington, D.C. 20009

Children's Foundation
1028 Connecticut Avenue, N.W.
Suite 1112
Washington, D.C. 20036

Closer Look: National Information Center for
the Handicapped
Box 1492
Washington, D.C. 20013

Council for Exceptional Children
1920 Association Drive
Retson, Virginia 22091

Council of National Organizations for Children
and Youth
1910 K Street, N.W.
Washington, D.C. 20005

Day Care and Child Development Council of
America
1401 K Street, N.W.
Washington, D.C. 20085

Down's Syndrome Congress
1709 Frederick Street
Cumberland, Maryland 21502

Education Commission of the States
Handicapped Children's Education Project
300 Lincoln Tower
1860 Lincoln Street
Denver, Colorado 80203

Epilepsy Foundation of America
1828 L Street, N.W.
Washington, D.C. 20036

Goodwill Industries of America
9200 Wisconsin Avenue
Washington, D.C. 20014

International Association of Parents of the Deaf
814 Thayer Avenue
Silver Spring, Maryland 20910

International League of Societies for the Mentally
Handicapped
rue Forestiere 12
B-1050
Brussels, Belgium

International Society for Rehabilitation of
the Disabled
219 East 44th Street
New York, New York 10017

Joseph P. Kennedy, Jr. Foundation
1701 K Street, N.W.
Suite 205
Washington, D.C. 20006

Library of Congress, Division for the Blind and
Physically Handicapped
Washington, D.C. 20542

Mental Health Law Project
1751 N Street, N.W.
Washington, D.C. 20036

Muscular Dystophy Associations of America
810 7th Avenue
New York, New York 10019

National Society for Prevention of
Blindness,Inc.
79 Madison Avenue
New York, New York 10016

The National Association for Gifted Children
8080 Springvalley Drive
Cincinnati, Ohio 45236

National Association for Mental Health
1800 North Kent Street
Arlington, Virginia 22209

National Association for Music Therapy
P.O. Box 610
Lawrence, Kansas 66044

National Association for Retarded Citizens
2709 Avenue E East
Arlington, Texas 76011

National Association of Coordinators of
State Programs for the Mentally Retarded
2001 Jefferson Davis Highway
Arlington, Virginia 22202

National Association of State Directors of
Special Education
1201 16th Street, N.W.
Washington, D.C. 20036

National Association of Private Residential
Facilities for the Mentally Retarded
6269 Leesburg Pike
Falls Church, Virginia 22044

National Association of Private Schools
for Exceptional Children
P.O. Box 928
Lake Wales, Florida 33853

National Association of Social Workers
2 Park Avenue
New York, New York 10016

National Ataxia Foundation
4225 Bolden Valley Road
Minneapolis, Minnesota 55422

National Center for Child Advocacy
U.S. Department of Health, Education and Welfare
Office of Child Development
P.O. Box 1182
Washington, D.C. 20013

National Center for Law and the Handicapped
1236 North Eddy Street
South Bend, Indiana 46617

National Center for Voluntary Action
1735 I Street, N.W.
Washington, D.C. 20006

National Center on Educational Media and
Materials for the Handicapped
Ohio State Unviersity
220 West 12th Avenue
Columbus, Ohio 43210

National Committee
Arts for the Handicapped
1701 K Street, N.W.
Suite 801
Washington, D.C. 20037

National Committee for Citizens in Education
410 Wilde Lake Village Green
Columbia, Maryland 21044

National Council of Community Mental Health
Centers
2233 Wisconsin Avenue, N.W.
Washington, D.C. 20007

National Council for the Gifted
700 Prospect Avenue
West Orange, New Jersey 07052

National Easter Seal Society for Crippled Children
and Adults
2023 West Ogden Avenue
Chicago, Illinois 60612

National Epilepsy League
116 South Michigan Avenue
Chicago, Illinois 60603

National Genetics Foundation
250 West 57th Street
New York, New York 10019

National Information and Referral Service for
Autistic and Autistic-like Persons
302 31st Street
Huntington, West Virginia 25702

National Institute on Mental Retardation
Kinsman NIMR Building
York University Campus
4700 Keele Street
Donsview (Toronoto)
Ontario, Canada M3J 1P3

National Paraplegia Foundation
333 North Michigan Avenue
Chicago, Illinois 60601

National Rehabilitation Association
1522 K Street, N.W.
Washington, D.C. 20005

National Society for Autistic Children
169 Tampa Avenue
Albany, New York 12208

National State Leadership Training Institute on
the Gifted and Talented
316 West Second Street (Suite PH-C)
Los Angeles, California 90012

National Tay-Sachs and Allied Diseases
Association, Room 1617
200 Park Avenue South
New York, New York 10003

Office of the Gifted
400 Maryland Avenue, S.W.
Washington, D.C. 20202

Orton Society
8415 Bellona Lane
Towson, Maryland 21204

Physical Education and Recreation
for the Handicapped: Information and
Research Utilization Center
1201 16th Street, N.W.
Washington, D.C. 20036

President's Committee on Employment
of the Handicapped
1111 20th Street, N.W.
Washington, D.C. 20010

President's Committee on Mental Retardation
Washington, D.C. 20201

Spina Bifida Association of America
P.O. Box G-1974
Elmhurst, Illinois 60126

Therapeutic Recreation Information Center
University of Oregon
1597 Agate Street
Eugene, Oregon 97403

United Cerebral Palsy Association
66 East 34th Street
New York, New York 10016

"Mainstream on Call"*
1-800-424-8089

*A toll free number for individuals to obtain
answers to questions about Federal legislation
concerning the handicapped.

STAFF

Publisher	John Quirk
Managing Director	John Sullivan
Editor	Roberta Garland
Director of Production	Richard Pawlikowski
Director of Design	Donald Burns
Typesetting	Carol Carr
Production Ass't	Mary Kirkiles
Cover Design	Donald Burns

ORDER FORM

_____ Administration of Special Education (8.75)
_____ Autism (8.75)
_____ Behavior Modification (8.75)
_____ Career & Vocational Education for the
            Handicapped (8.75)
_____ Child Abuse (8.75)
_____ Child Psychology (8.75)
_____ Classroom Teacher & Special Education (8.75)
_____ Counseling Parents of Exceptional Children (8.75)
_____ Curriculum Development for the Gifted (8.75)
_____ Deaf Education (8.75)
_____ Diagnosis & Placement (8.75)
_____ Down's Syndrome (8.75)
_____ Dyslexia (8.75)
_____ Early Childhood Education (8.75)
_____ Educable Mentally Handicapped (8.75)
_____ Emotional & Behavior Disorders (8.75)
_____ Foundations of Gifted Educations (8.75)
_____ Gifted & Talented Education (8.75)

_____ Hyperactivity (8.75)
_____ Individualized Education Program (8.75)
_____ Instructional Media & Special Education (8.75)
_____ Law & Special Education: Due Process (8.75)
_____ Learning Disabilities (8.75)
_____ Mainstreaming (8.75)
_____ Mental Retardation (8.75)
_____ Physically Handicapped (8.75)
_____ Pre-school Education for the Handicapped (8.75)
_____ Psychology of Exceptional Children (small) (8.75)
_____ Psychology of Exceptional Children (large) (19.95)
_____ Severely & Profoundly Handicapped (8.75)
_____ Special Education (8.75)
_____ Special Olympics (8.75)
_____ Speech & Hearing (8.75)
_____ Trainable Mentally Handicapped (8.75)
_____ Visually Handicapped Education (8.75)
_____ Vocational Training for the Mentally Retarded (8.75)

_____ Abnormal Psychology: Problems of Disordered Emotional & Behavioral
            Development (8.75)

_____ Development Psychology: The Problems of Disordered Mental
            Development (8.75)

_____ Human Growth & Development of Exceptional Individual (8.75)

1. Orders will not be processed without _complete_ mailing address, including _zip code._
2. Orders not accompanied by a purchase order number must be prepaid.
3. Orders under $15. must be accompanied by check. Add 10% shipping & handling.
4. Orders less that $100., add 10% shipping & handling.
5. Orders over $100., add 2% handling, shipping will be charged via specific rate.
6. Orders of 5 or more of one title receive 20% discount, less than five will be billed at catalog price.

Checks payable to: SPECIAL LEARNING CORPORATION
Allow 3-6 weeks for 4th Class (book rate) delivery

BUSINESS REPLY MAIL

First Class Permit No. 142- Guilford

Postage will be paid by addressee

SPECIAL LEARNING CORP.
P.O. Box 306
Guilford, CT. 06437

SPECIAL LEARNING CORPORATION

COMMENTS PLEASE ! ! !

1. Where did you use this book?

2. In what course or workshop did you use this reader?

3. What articles did you find most interesting and useful?

4. Have you read any articles that we should consider including in this reader?

5. What other features would you like to see added?

6. Should the format be changed, what would you like to see changed?

7. In what other area would you like us to publish using this format?

8. Did you use this as a
( ) basic text?   ( ) in-service?
( ) supplement?   ( ) general information?

———————————————— Fold Here ————————————————

Are you a ( ) student ( ) instructor ( ) teacher ( ) parent

Your Name _____

School _____

School address _____

_____

Home Address _____

City _____ St. _____ Zip _____

Telephone Number _____

TM/H

☐   **ORDER PLACED ON REVERSE SIDE**